The Rebirth of Live
The Eldonian V

The Rebirth of Liverpool
The Eldonian Way

JACK McBANE

LIVERPOOL UNIVERSITY PRESS

First published 2008 by
Liverpool University Press
4 Cambridge Street
Liverpool, L69 7ZU

British Library Cataloguing-in-Publication Data
A British Library CIP Record is available

ISBN 978-1-84631-164-2 hb
978-1-84631-158-1 pb

Publication supported by the Academy for Sustainable Communities

Typeset in Adobe Jensen by Koinonia, Manchester
Printed and bound by Gutenberg Press, Malta

Contents

To our sons and grandsons – Joe, Will, Owen, Ben and Henry
– may you always have love…

Acknowledgements

THIS BOOK WAS commissioned by The Eldonian Community Trust and sponsored by the Academy for Sustainable Communities, with additional contributions from the Eldonian Community-Based Housing Association, Vicinity Housing Group and Riverside Housing.

It has been a real joy to revisit the Eldonians and their story after so many years, so my first thanks are to them, particularly, those who I interviewed. I also want to thank those people who read and made helpful comments on early drafts of the chapters. They include Tony McGann, George Evans, Julie Backhouse, Peter Roberts, Bill Halsall and Max Steinberg.

It has been good fun searching for photos and information related to the story, and in this respect, my particular thanks to: Tony Hall of the *Liverpool Echo* who delved into their archives to provide me with early press cuttings and photographs; David Jewell for all his photographs; the Halsall/Lloyd Partnership for their photos and illustrations; and Liverpool Record Office, Mills Media Ltd and Webb Aviation for supplying photographs.

Finally, this book would not have been written but for the roles played by Jane McBane, my wife. First, she prompted me to contact Tony McGann to remind him it was time to get their story told. Her research skills and experience were invaluable in the design of the project, including the interviews. Most significantly, she has edited, reworked and polished the original text every step of the way. Lastly, she spent countless hours transcribing all the interviews, which included coping with the Liverpool accent!

Foreword

I AM PROUD to write this foreword to the story of the Eldonians of Liverpool. The Eldonian Village has been thirty years in the making. In 1977 this neighbourhood faced demolition through slum clearance and the community was to be broken up. But rather than accepting their fate, the individuals and families who made up the old neighbourhood decided to remain together and to work together to create a new neighbourhood – one they could be proud of.

Thirty years on, all those who have worked so hard to make the village what it is today can be proud of their work. When I visited last year, I was struck by the progress that had been made and the beacon to other communities across the country that the Eldonian Village has become.

The commitment and strong leadership of Tony McGann, who has worked so hard for over thirty years for his community, has been an inspiration in this success story and deserves particular mention. The work done by Tony and so many others over these past years is, for me, a model for what can be achieved when communities pull together, and for the new Britain we are striving to achieve. Communities where all families who work hard can build a better life for themselves and their children; where everyone should rise as far as their talents can take them; and where the talents of each of us should contribute to the well being of all.

That is why I am delighted to pay tribute to the Eldonians and all the people who have worked with them over thirty years. This book tells their story in the words of those who played their part in its unfolding. We have all much to learn from it.

Gordon Brown
Prime Minister

Introduction

IN 1987 A NEIGHBOURHOOD in the north docklands of Liverpool won the Times/RIBA[1] award as the most outstanding example of community enterprise in the UK. In August 2004 the United Nations granted the same community a World Habitat Award, a first for any community in the UK. In 2005 the community was chosen by the British Urban Regeneration Association as one of the best examples of regeneration in the UK between 1990 and 2005. And today, in a succession of independent academic and professional evaluations, this neighbourhood has been recognized as a sustainable community and as a model for other neighbourhoods facing restructuring.

Back in 1978 this neighbourhood was a slum with tenements awaiting demolition. The people living there had survived poverty and poor housing since many of their ancestors' arrival from Ireland in the middle of the nineteenth century; they had survived bombings during the Second World War; they had survived the building of the new Mersey Tunnel through their neighbourhood; they had survived a ring road; and they had survived loss of jobs with the closure of the docks and local industry.

The neighbourhood is Vauxhall and the neighbours are the Eldonians. What happened between 1978 and 2004 to bring about such a dramatic transformation? This book is the story of the people and their place, in their own words. It is about how they, 'with a little help from their friends', have created a world-class, vibrant, sustainable community.

Theirs is a unique achievement in the history of social housing and urban

1 Royal Institute of British Architects.

Tony McGann, Chairman of the Eldonians, receiving the Times/RIBA award from Prince Charles

regeneration. They live in a model inner city village that they own and manage. But they are not yet finished. They have further ambitious plans for their area, and they offer advice to other communities throughout the UK and the world.

The first few chapters of this book focus on this remarkable village as it is today, why the Eldonians have won the acclaim of the United Nations and why they are recognized as a model sustainable community. In Section II, the focus turns to the historical context for this community, which is vital to understand its approach and motivation. Section III recounts the Eldonian story – what they did and how they did it – mainly in the words of the people who made it happen. The concluding chapter speculates on what can be learned from their achievements.

I

The Eldonians Today, A Sustainable Community

The Eldonian Village Today

1

THE ELDONIAN VILLAGE is in the Vauxhall area of Liverpool, about a quarter of a mile north of the city centre and close to the docks. When the first phase of the village was completed in 1989, it was an oasis surrounded by derelict land and run-down housing that had not yet been reclaimed and redeveloped. Such was the commitment of the residents even then that they *knew* this was home and that, eventually, further redevelopment would come. Today, despite continuing deprivation in north Liverpool, it no longer stands out as an oasis because the whole of the Vauxhall area is in the process of redevelopment with investment from the public, private and community sectors.

What type of organization is it?

The Eldonian organization has three elements:

- A Community Trust, a registered charity run by elected local people, directing all elements of the organization.
- The Eldonian Group, delivering physical, economic and training projects to help bring economic sustainability for the community.
- The Community-Based Housing Association (CBHA), registered with the Housing Corporation as a social landlord, and providing affordable social housing for the community, elderly care facilities and management for leaseholders who have bought apartments in the city centre.

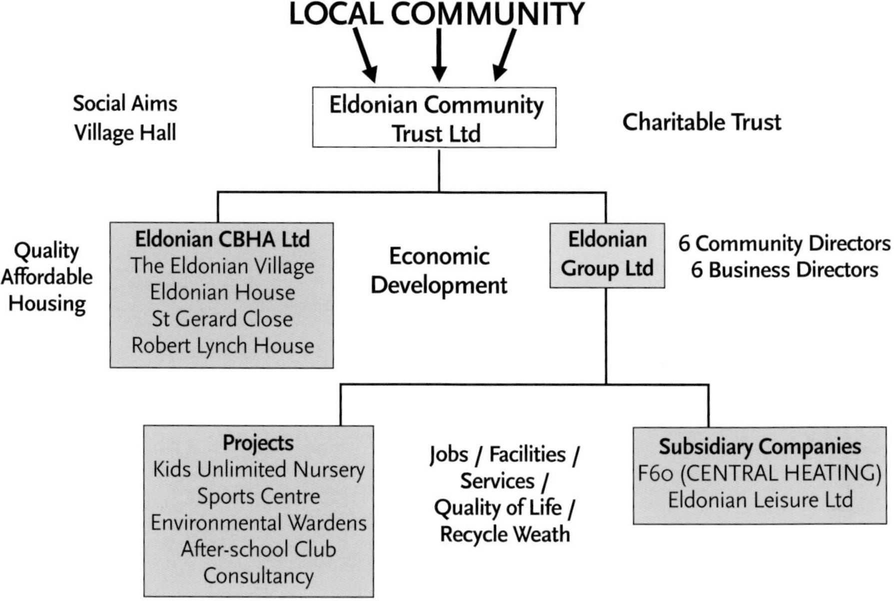

The management structure of the Eldonian organization

Local people govern all parts of the organization. In total, over one hundred people are employed in all aspects of the organization, most of whom come from the area.

The Community Trust

The Trust is the overarching organization and represents the whole community of over 2,500 people. It was formed in 1987 with objectives to advance education, to provide facilities for leisure and recreation and to provide residential accommodation for elderly people in the village.

The Eldonian Group

The Group is a Development Trust, employing over fifty people and led by its Chief Executive, Lawrence Santangeli. It has a range of economic services that are offered to people in the area and in other parts of the UK. Current services include business support to small firms and social enterprises, including advice to organizations wanting to tender for public service contracts. It operates a number of social enterprises – managing a sports centre, an environmental

The management committee of the Community-Based Housing Association

maintenance business, gas central heating servicing and installation – and is currently involved with developers for a new £90m scheme in Vauxhall.

The Community-Based Housing Association (CBHA)

The CBHA started life as the Eldonian Housing Cooperative in 1984. It developed and managed Phase 1 of the village on the former site of a Tate & Lyle sugar refinery. In the 1990s it changed into a community-based housing association to allow it to work in the wider area and to enter into partnerships with private developers.

Tenants make up 75 per cent of the management board, which is elected annually by members at the Annual General Meeting. The board through its Chair, Tony McGann, employs the management team. The Director of Housing is George Evans, who has a team of fifteen people who are responsible for the day-to-day management of the 523 properties for which the association has responsibility. Of the 523 properties, the CBHA owns 376 and manages 147 on behalf of owner occupiers. As of 2007, the CBHA has an annual turnover of some £1.5m and has assets of close to £10m. The association trains and employs local people in housing and estate management. The elderly accommodation is managed mainly by local people. A small maintenance team, also local people, carries out communal landscaping and small repairs throughout the village.

The Eldonians also pioneered a pilot 'parish wardens' scheme, financed by the CBHA. It was partly this example that led the government to fund neighbourhood wardens across the UK. The Eldonians Neighbourhood Warden Scheme was run by the Eldonian Group until the government

Aerial view of the Eldonian Village as it is today

withdrew funding nationally in favour of community safety officers under the control of the police. The Group then reconfigured the team to create environmental wardens who provide gardening services, graffiti removal and other stewardship services under contract to the wider area. The latest project along these lines are the canal wardens, again employed via the Group, who provide environmental services on the canal towpaths and surrounds.

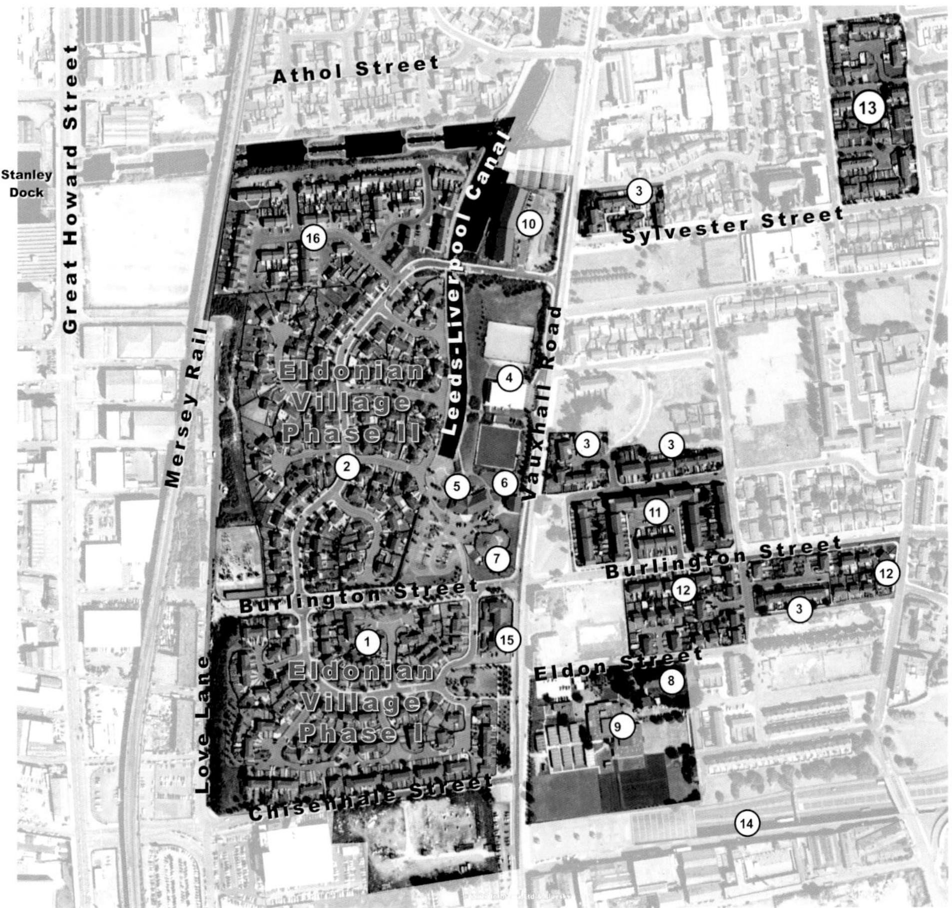

The key sites in the village

1. Phase 1 Eldonian Village
2. Phase 2 Eldonian Village
3. Portland Gardens Co-op Scheme
4. Elaine Norris Sports Centre
5. Eldonian Village Hall
6. Tony McGann Centre
7. Kids Unlimited Nursery
8. Our Lady's Church
9. Our Lady's School
10. Robert Lynch House
11. Portland Gardens Conversion
12. Site of former Eldon Street and Burlington Street tenements
13. Hopwood Ashfield Development
14. Mersey Tunnel Kingsway
15. Eldonian House
16. Private Sector Development

In the 2006 Annual Report of the CBHA, George Evans, the Director of Housing, explained that the Housing Corporation, their regulator, had awarded them three 'green lights'. This means that the Corporation has no concerns regarding the viability, governance and management of the association and considers it to be a low-risk organization.

What is in the village?

The village today is a mix of housing and facilities to ensure that everyone in the community, from the cradle to the grave, is catered for and belongs. The Eldonians' initial aim was to keep the community together in new, decent, affordable housing within this part of the Vauxhall area and to give themselves a greater say in their future. As their skills and aspirations grew, they realized that more was required to enable people of all ages to stay in the area for the long term. So they set about developing broader housing and care facilities.

Although this is one unified village, the Eldonians themselves see it as the result of two main phases of development. The description below is a brief picture of the village following those two phases. How these developments came about is covered in Section III of this book.

Phase 1 of the Eldonian Village housing project

The first houses to be built in the current village were completed in 1989 – 145 houses and bungalows, including specific designs for older people and people with disabilities. These were for the people from the condemned council tenements on Burlington and Eldon Streets, and it was the closure of the nearby Tate & Lyle sugar refinery in 1981 that provided a site large enough to accommodate them. The community approached the government for support and eventually secured £6.6m of grants to purchase part of the Tate & Lyle site for reclamation and new housing. Each house and garden was designed to the requirements of the initial occupants, resulting in a neighbourhood with over 28 different house types.

This was not the first housing project of the Eldonians, but it was the first to result in homes owned and managed within the community. Their earlier project is a significant factor in their story and features later in the book.

While their own site was being developed, the Eldonians also helped a small group of local elderly residents to construct purpose-built bungalows

Before: Sheehan Heights, where the 15 elderly residents lived

After: The new scheme facilitated by the Eldonians

The refurbished Leeds/Liverpool canal looking towards the city centre

Eldonian House residential care home

on St Gerard Close. The new homes replaced their semi-derelict tower block, Sheehan Heights, just north of the village; they were completed in 1990 and are managed by the CBHA.

Phase 2 of the housing project: the extended village

By 1994 the Eldonians had built another 150 homes around or directly facing the Leeds/Liverpool canal. The canal was de-contaminated, re-oriented, landscaped and brought back into active use with the help of British Waterways, reversing more than a century of industrial use, tipping, pollution and disrepair. Again the housing features a range of different designs and house types and is now occupied mainly by younger families.

The Eldonians achieved this development by securing the rest of the former Tate & Lyle site in 1991, followed by £5.5m grant from the Housing Corporation and a £1.5m loan raised from the Cooperative Bank. This phase of the village development contributed greatly to the sustainability and overall future of the Eldonian community.

Two other developments in this phase were the Eldonian House, a 30-room residential care home for elderly people, built in 1991 with the help of Merseyside Improved Houses housing association (now called Riverside Housing) and the Housing Corporation. This proved to be a significant milestone for the community, offering residents the opportunity to stay within their community in dignity and comfort, and close to their families. The home is approved by Liverpool City Council for the care of elderly people and has recently been modified and re-registered, so that 15 of the rooms are now used by elderly mentally infirm residents, including those suffering with Alzheimer's disease.

A second development was Robert Lynch House, completed in 2006. This is an extra-care sheltered scheme, with 36 self-contained flats for older people and 24-hour cover. Bobby Lynch is a local resident who worked for elderly people in the community over many years. He was also a home visitor for the charity Age Concern, visiting elderly victims of crime and fitting safety chains and spyholes to their property.

Through all of these housing developments the environment is a key feature. There are high-quality open spaces. The imaginative use of landscaping and of the canal as the core of the village further contribute to a sense of well-being and liberation from high-density urban living.

Robert Lynch House: extra-care sheltered scheme

Part of the new environment, forming a buffer with Vauxhall Road

And what of the future? A key priority is to attract young homeowners into the area, bringing additional spending power with them. With this in mind, current projects in 2007 include a joint scheme with Liverpool Housing Trust to build 36 apartments for sale in the village and further new housing on land adjacent to the village.

Beyond housing

From the outset the Eldonians had a long-term vision to regenerate their entire neighbourhood. While the first priorities were to resolve their terrible housing problems, they knew that a neighbourhood was about more than houses. They realized that to make a community sustainable, it is necessary to improve health, education and employment. It is also critical to ensure that it is a safe place to live or run a business. They also recognized that the community was not just those who lived in the social housing; it included everyone who lived in the area, including owner occupiers; it included everyone who had a business in the area; and it included the local schools, doctors and other services.

In 1982, with the help of their professional advisors, they developed their vision for what was called a Self-Regenerating Community. It was initially intended for submission for an ideas competition for local land, and it was modified from time to time, but it was the foundation and driver for forward planning and development work for the next twenty years. It was in effect a 'master plan' as it had ideas for environmental improvements, local shops, social and recreational facilities and mixed tenure housing.

Once the first new housing developments were approved, the Eldonians turned their attention to these other aspects of their self-regenerating community. In 1987 they established the development trust (the Eldonian Group) to take forward facilities and plans that were 'beyond housing'. The facilities in the village today, arising from the work of the Group, are described below.

The Tony McGann Centre, an office complex, accommodates the CBHA staff who are employed by and responsible to the community. It is used by all the Eldonian organizations and by tenants seeking advice and support.

The Eldonian Village Hall, completed in 1993, is a meeting place, pub and social venue for all the community and is situated on the Eldonian Basin. It employs local people, hosts local groups, events and charitable functions, and serves as an attraction for canal-users, especially during the annual Mersey

The Tony McGann Centre and offices for the CBHA

River Festival. The village hall is a thriving community business. It is owned by the Community Trust, and a proportion of its annual profits are ploughed back into the community to help fund local activities.

Kids Unlimited Day Nursery opened in 1994 and is a 50-place nursery for children aged from three months to five years. Built in partnership with the private-sector Littlewoods organization and with assistance from the then Merseyside Development Corporation, the nursery offers childcare facilities for the local community and the wider business community. Today it is owned outright by the Eldonian Group.

The Elaine Norris Sports Centre opened in 1998 in response to the health needs of the community of north Liverpool. It was named in memory of Elaine Norris, an active board member of the Trust until she died in 1995. It offers sports and leisure opportunities for all ages, including a bowling green, a five-a-side football pitch, multi-gym, sauna facility and steam room, as well as playing host to canal boaters. It is also the base for the Eldonians' youth activities.

The Village Hall – in the centre of the community

A friendly game of bowls behind the Village Hall

Kids Unlimited: The 50-place nursery that was a partnership and is now owned by the Eldonian Group

The Elaine Norris Sports Hall

Phase 3 – beyond the boundaries

The Eldonians have now moved beyond the physical boundary of the village. They are committed to sharing best practice and to making an impact on the wider area. This work is in full partnership with the private sector, other community and voluntary groups, and statutory regeneration agencies.

The most significant proposal in 2007 is for a £90m joint private-sector scheme for the Vauxhall Road corridor, to provide new shops, offices, leisure facilities, restaurants and bars alongside more than 400 new houses and apartments, some of which will be aimed at first-time buyers. The proposed site is also close to the Eldonian Village, between Pall Mall and Vauxhall Road. At the time of writing, public consultation has begun.

Such a large private investment in their area brings obvious benefits, including much-needed provision for local shopping. Equally importantly, the Eldonian Group is negotiating for local people to manage many of the services in the new complex, including property and neighbourhood services, concierge services, car parks, crèche and café.

Another significant development is a new extension of the Leeds/Liverpool canal, built by British Waterways, from the village into the centre of Liverpool. This will open in 2008. The canal was first opened in Liverpool in

The proposed new development with a private developer Viride

1777 for transporting goods. When the Tate & Lyle sugar refinery opened in Vauxhall in 1872, it put the canal to good use until motor transport made it redundant. In the latter part of the twentieth century the canal was abandoned and left as derelict for many years. When the Eldonian Village was extended into Phase 2, the Eldonians decided to reclaim and restore that part of the canal in the new development, and it is now the centrepiece of the village. The success of the village and the beauty and safety of the canal have now attracted canal boat users back into Liverpool.

Other projects include:

- developing an Enterprise Park project with industrial units and managed workspace for both existing employers and for new businesses;
- developing targeted job training schemes across the north Liverpool area to improve employment skills and experience and to develop employee confidence and self-esteem;

Stanley Dock Lock Flight

Part of the Eldon Wharf estate of private housing and the start of the canal extension

- setting up their own Social Enterprise Development Service to help other communities to develop businesses;
- extending the model and sharing best practice through hosting visitors and accepting invitations from other interested groups from across the world to attend conferences;
- providing consultancy services in housing areas in London and the north-east of England.

In summary, the Eldonians have been an 'anchor' for the whole of the Vauxhall area since they commenced in the late 1970s. If they had not fought to keep their community together in 1978, it is quite likely that the land on which the Eldonian Village is located today would be a bland business park, a multi-storey car park for people working in the city centre, or worse, an abandoned derelict and contaminated site. Instead, they have kept the area alive with people who love to live there.

As a result of their success, new private investment in Liverpool city centre is coming out to their neighbourhood. They have turned their part of Vauxhall into a desirable place to live, and developers even use the Eldonian name and reputation to sell their houses!

What separates the Eldonians from many other neighbourhoods across the UK that have successfully provided new houses for local people? Most neighbourhood organizations, including housing cooperatives, fight only for the development of new houses. In most cases, this may be a reasonable outcome, given the local circumstances. Indeed, Liverpool itself has a large number of new-build housing cooperatives that built new houses and then stopped, and most are now managed by housing associations. What set the Eldonians apart was their willingness in the early days to adopt a wider vision for the whole of their neighbourhood.

2 A Sustainable Community

A GREAT STORY is not worth much if it cannot be shared with other people, and the Eldonian story is no exception. There are lessons from their achievements for other neighbourhoods, professionals, agencies, governments and those learning about regeneration and sustainability.

The Academy for Sustainable Communities was launched by the British government in February 2005. It is the national centre of excellence for the skills and knowledge needed to create sustainable communities. The Academy's work focuses on three main areas: increasing skills and learning, targeting skills shortages and sharing knowledge and expertise.

The Academy has developed a model for a sustainable community, which includes eight key components that make up the ideal neighbourhood. The components are retrospectively applied to places that have undergone regeneration, and when they are all present in a neighbourhood, the Academy believes that they combine to make 'a place'.

In a review of the Eldonian Village, the chair of the Academy for Sustainable Communities, Professor Peter Roberts, provides a helpful explanation of the origins of the term 'sustainable communities' as distinct from regeneration, and why the key components are important.[1] He argues that regeneration in

1 Peter Roberts, 'Social Innovation, Spatial Transformation and Sustainable Communities: Liverpool and the Eldonians', in P. Drewe, E. Hulsbergen and J. Klein (eds), *The Challenge of Social Innovation in Urban Revitalisation* (Techne Press, 2007), pp. 117–33. Further academic assessments of the Eldonian Village include Richard Meegan and Alison Mitchell, 'It's Not Community Round Here, It's Neighbourhood', *Urban Studies*, 38.12 (2001), 2167–94; and Karen Leeming, 'Sustainable Urban Development: A Case Study of "the Eldonians" in Liverpool', in Tasleem Shakur (ed.), *Cities in Transition: Transforming the Global Built Environment* (Open House Press, 2005).

itself, i.e. improving a place that has failed, is not sufficient. Having regenerated a place, it is critical to continue with improvements and to ensure that the place is managed as a 'sustainable community'.

The sustainable communities policy and practice, therefore, go beyond regeneration. First, they seek to apply a comprehensive set of theoretical and practical principles to the creation and management of *new* places as well as old in order to ensure they are well established and managed over the long term:

> Given that regeneration activity is concerned with dealing with the problems encountered in places that have experienced some form of market failure... then it is both inappropriate and somewhat illogical to refer to the creation and management of new places by using the same term.[2]

Secondly, sustainable communities' policy and practice are concerned with place and 'place-making'. Deep-rooted problems in neighbourhoods cannot be addressed by regeneration initiatives that are limited in time, scope or funding. The eight key components of the sustainable community model together reflect the objective of creating places where people want to live, now and in the future – in other words, 'place-making'.

Does the Eldonian Village match up to the eight key components of sustainability? In the same chapter cited above, Peter Roberts concludes that it does.

Why the Eldonian Village is a sustainable community

An active, inclusive and safe place

> *...inclusive, offer a sense of community identity and belonging, be tolerant, offer respect, be friendly and cooperative and provide opportunities for culture, leisure and sport*[3]

The way in which the Eldonians created their village both illustrated and reinforced their sense of community identity and belonging. The first phase of the Eldonian Village has 145 homes and 28 house types. Bill Halsall, their

2 Roberts, 'Social Innovation', 120.

3 Roberts, 'Social Innovation', 123.

architect, worked closely for over twelve months with the people who were to move there, to shape their houses and the layout to accommodate their particular needs. He created his own adult education programme with tools and models to give people the ability to 'design'. This included trips to see other housing schemes that helped people to create a vision for their own place. Everyone had to approve the final design of his or her house. This was the essential principle of the Eldonians: everyone will be included.

Bill's work was pioneering and very effective. People with no experience of architecture and planning became empowered to play an active role in the process of shaping their own neighbourhood. It eventually became known as 'planning for real', although at that time Bill and his colleagues had no template to work from.

The sense of belonging is further illustrated by the way elderly people have been provided for over the years. The first generation of residents had houses and bungalows. The Eldonians were quick to realize the need to plan for accommodation for their ageing residents, so that they did not have to move away from the area – which, of course, was what their original struggle was all about. So they built a care home, the Eldonian House, described in Chapter 1. Inevitably, as time passed, some of the residents required more specialized help. So, always able to react quickly to the needs of the community, the CBHA modified the building and re-registered the home so that 15 flats could be used by elderly mentally infirm residents. This ensured that such residents would not have to move out of their home to receive the help and care they needed.

Again, it became evident recently that more was needed for the older people in the area. Local Authorities were closing sheltered schemes; private nursing homes were being sold as owners took advantage of rising house and land prices; and the future funding for care was uncertain and inadequate. As no one else was prepared to take up the challenge, the Eldonians once again decided to do it themselves. With help from the Housing Corporation, a loan, and meeting the shortfall from their own reserves, they set about providing another facility for the community. So in 2006 Robert Lynch House, the extra-care sheltered scheme described in Chapter 1, was opened.

The Eldonians have also always recognized the value of enjoying leisure time together. While they were still living in the tenements, they were very attached to their social club, called the Jubilee Club or Our Lady's. While it was not the most attractive building, it provided people with a place to meet and socialize, and it was where most of the plans were drawn up for the new village across the road. It followed that the new village would also have its own social club. The new club is a very busy centre for the whole community to meet and enjoy themselves. It is literally in the middle of the village, very attractively designed and situated adjacent to the reclaimed Leeds/Liverpool canal.

Leisure and sport are catered for in the sports centre, with a gym and keep-fit facilities, an artificial turf bowling green and football pitches. Finally, they have provided for the very young within the area, with the 50-place nursery described in Chapter 1.

Well run

> *...enjoy representative and accountable governance with strategic and visionary leadership, strong and effective partnerships, effective engagement with the community, a strong and inclusive voluntary and community sector, and a sense of civic values and responsibility*[4]

The formal structure and decision-making process of the Eldonians was explained in Chapter 1. The CBHA is a model organization according to the Housing Corporation, its regulator, and is regarded as 'low risk'. As with all healthy public sector organizations, the boards have a range of skills including experts from the private sector in Liverpool. New recruits to the board are provided with induction and training, and are supported by the staff while they settle in.

In the 1980s the community was struggling for survival, and the only partners they sought were allies, professional and personal, to help them. As they have grown in confidence and reputation, they have become active and skilled partners with both the private and public sectors, as will become clear as their story unfolds.

Residents of the village have a strong sense of civic pride, not often found in inner city areas in the UK. People respect each other, aggressive behaviour is not tolerated and the care of residents is paramount to the team that runs the CBHA.

4 Roberts, 'Social Innovation', 123.

Environmentally sensitive

> *...actively seek to minimise climate change, protect the environment, minimise waste, make efficient use of natural resources, protect bio-diversity, minimise negative environmental impact and create cleaner, safer, greener neighbourhoods*[5]

The village was designed in the 1980s and 1990s and was funded by the government. At that time there was less concern with climate change and environmental impact than today, and there were also fewer funds available to design-in environmentally friendly measures. Despite this, the residents and Bill Halsall, their architect, achieved a number of successes, including:

- re-use of brownfield land that was reclaimed with the removal of pollutants;
- an enhanced bio-diversity through landscape planting and reclamation of the Leeds/Liverpool canal;
- designs that incorporated energy efficiency in the dwellings through cavity wall and loft insulation;
- use of doors and windows that are weather efficient;
- use of recycled materials such as granite setts, and sand dredged from the Mersey for the site foundations.

Well-designed and built

> *...a sense of place, user friendly green spaces, a sufficient range of affordable and accessible housing, excellent buildings; appropriate layout, density and design; buildings and public spaces which promote health and which are safe; accessible jobs and services by public transport, walking and cycling*[6]

The design of the whole village reflects what people wanted and what was affordable. In those early days not one of the original 145 families had ever had a garden or internal stairs! In later phases the Eldonians secured funding for the other facilities that go to make up a 'place' – the sports centre, social club, bowls green, artificial turf football park and pleasant open green spaces. These facilities are carefully integrated into the village.

5 Roberts, 'Social Innovation', 123.

6 Roberts, 'Social Innovation', 123.

The Eldonians were among the first to involve the police in trying to design crime out of their village, a practice that is now commonplace. The house designs and street layouts of the village were informed by experts from Merseyside Police, who now use the Eldonian Village as an example of best practice when presenting 'safe by design' seminars to professionals and developers. Their attention to safety and 'looking out for each other' means that it is not possible to walk around the village without being overlooked by a number of houses.

Well-connected

> *...transport facilities that reduce dependence on cars, facilities for safe walking and cycling, appropriate local parking, available telecommunications and good access to regional, national and international networks*[7]

The village is on Vauxhall Road, a main thoroughfare into the centre of the city. The city centre is a 10-minute walk away. Car ownership is below average due to levels of income and the number of older residents. Adequate parking is designed for each house and is provided for visitors to the club and the other facilities. Phase 2 of the development of the village reclaimed the abandoned Leeds/Liverpool canal. The canal is the central feature of the village and offers attractive and safe places for walking and cycling. In 2007 British Waterways, which is responsible for the UK's canal system, commenced an extension of the canal from the village into the city centre.

Thriving

> *... a wide range of jobs and training opportunities, sufficient land and buildings to support economic activity, dynamic job and business creation, a strong business community, and economically viable and attractive town centres*[8]

Within the village, the Eldonians have a number of successful social enterprises that train and employ local people. These include the housing association, the maintenance team, environmental wardens, canal wardens, the nursery, the social club and the homes for elderly people. Increasing private investment is coming into Vauxhall, partly due to the financial success of the

7 Roberts, 'Social Innovation', 123.

8 Roberts, 'Social Innovation', 123.

Eldonian Village, with the related increase in land values, and the regeneration of Liverpool centre.

As described in Chapter 1, the Eldonians are active partners with the private sector for new developments in their area. These include more housing accommodation, business start-up centres, office developments and shops. Developers regularly approach them to participate in new investments that will bring new jobs and economic viability.

However, communities cannot be expected to be the drivers of economic regeneration. This must be led by the private sector as well as public agencies. Successful communities are those that are asked to participate in the process of economic regeneration, including becoming an investor, like the Eldonians.

Well-served

> *... good schools, colleges and universities and opportunities for lifelong learning, high quality local health, social and family services, a good range of affordable public, community, voluntary and private services, and service providers who think and act long-term and beyond their own immediate boundaries*[9]

The Vauxhall area now has a range of educational facilities, including the Kids Unlimited Nursery with 50 places, an 'out of school' club, a new 500-place junior and infant school, a comprehensive school that is a bus ride away and a new Community College. The latter was attracted into the neighbourhood by the Eldonians. The college is for 14 to 19 year olds and offers them training in building and construction. Liverpool has three excellent universities: Liverpool John Moores University, the University of Liverpool and Liverpool Hope University. Parts of John Moores are located on the fringes of Vauxhall.

Health facilities include a neighbourhood health centre with five GPs and a range of clinics. The Eldonians are in the planning stages for a new health centre for children on land on which they have an option to build. Their partners include a major Liverpool hospital, the city council and a private developer. They also provide residential health care for the elderly in their two homes in the village.

The Eldonians recognize the ongoing needs for improving educational attainment and higher levels of health for the people living in their neighbourhood. These two areas are central to their long-term goals, and discussions

9 Roberts, 'Social Innovation', 123.

are ongoing to develop new partnerships that will lead to projects on these fronts.

Fair for everyone

> *...recognise the rights and responsibilities of individuals, respect the rights and aspirations of others also to be sustainable; and have due regard to the needs of the future generations in current decisions and actions*[10]

The Eldonians are a caring, inclusive and democratic organization. They know their most valuable resource is their people and, of course, it is the people who live there who ultimately make the decisions. They know that there is more to be done to ensure the long-term prosperity of their neighbourhood. As we have seen, new developments are in the pipeline and more are on the drawing board.

Winner of the World Habitat Award 2004

Perhaps the ultimate recognition of a sustainable community is to be chosen by the United Nations as a 'World Habitat'. In 2004 the Eldonians received this recognition. What is the annual World Habitat Award and why did the Eldonians win it? It was established in 1985 by the UK-based Building and Social Housing Foundation as part of its contribution to the United Nations International Year of Shelter for the Homeless. Two awards are given each year to projects from the northern hemisphere and the southern hemisphere. The projects must provide practical and innovative solutions that come from within a community to their current housing needs and problems. Entry is open to individuals, organizations, local authorities and governments worldwide. The two winners receive their awards at the annual United Nations global celebration of World Habitat Day.

The Building and Social Housing Foundation also works to ensure that the ideas and approaches developed in the winning projects are widely shared. They organize international study groups, as well as publishing and disseminating information in a range of formats. Details of the winners over the years can be found on their website – www.bshf.org – all demonstrating the prestige of the award as well as the range of imaginative solutions to local housing problems.

10 Roberts, 'Social Innovation', 123.

President Mwai Kibaki of Kenya presenting Tony McGann and George Evans with the World Habitat Award

In their appraisal of the Eldonian Village for the World Habitat Award, the assessors made the following comments:

> The success of the Eldonian Village… is testimony to its long term sustainability, and it has deservedly become an internationally recognised model of community-led sustainable urban regeneration. Built to the current building standards and upgraded to improve resource efficiency, the housing is designed to contribute to environmental sustainability…
>
> An emphasis on local training and the creation of local employment has provided a boost to the economy. Small and medium enterprises are thriving and encouraging major companies into the area… A Neighbourhood Warden Scheme, alongside careful design and management strategies has enabled crime and anti social behaviour to be minimised in the area, creating safe and accessible space for all residents…
>
> A focus on the broader community has ensured that facilities and opportunities exist for all ages in the local community.[11]

11 Diane Diacon and Silvia Guimarães, *Presentation of the World Habitat Awards* (Building and Social Housing Foundation, 2004), 20–21.

Finally, the assessors highlighted the key elements of success, emphasizing similar features to the key components agreed by the British government's Academy for Sustainable Communities. In October 2004 Tony McGann and George Evans, on behalf of the Eldonians, went to Kenya to receive their award from Mwai Kibaki, the President of Kenya.

George has been working with and for the Eldonians longer than anyone. He was initially a senior officer at Liverpool City Council Housing Department and covered the Vauxhall area. He came to work with them from this job and is now the Director of Housing of the Eldonian Village. When asked why he thought they had won such a prestigious award, he said 'because every step of what we did was normal and can be replicated. I think what I'm doing is what every housing manager should do; it's nothing out of the normal for me, but to others it apparently is.'

He and Tony also asked the organizers of the award the same question. George takes up the story:

> Tony and I were invited to Kenya to receive the award on behalf of our community. The ceremony was to take place on the United Nations World Habitat Day, and had previously taken place in official buildings or palaces. On this occasion the organizers decided to hold the event in Kibera, the largest slum settlement in Kenya. All the dignitaries were transported to Kibera flanked by armed guards. When we arrived we witnessed the worst housing conditions that could ever be imagined – 750,000 people were living in corrugated huts spread as far as the eye could see. We were told that the settlement had no toilet facilities or proper sanitation. Tony and I just looked at each other trying to take in the deprivation laid out before us, and we thought 'Why are we here? These people should get the award for existing in these conditions.' So later, at the official reception, Tony asked the organizers why we got the award.
>
> The reply was that the award is less about what is built and more about sustainability and about ideas that, brought back to their basic form, will work anywhere because they are simple. The official went on to say that people living in poor conditions need to take control of their lives and to understand that their priorities include housing, health, education, employment and safety, and 'if there's no one else prepared to do it for you, be prepared to take it on yourself'.

Tony McGann and his local community *were* prepared to take it on themselves. But I will come to this in the main story.

Conclusion

The people who live in the Eldonian Village have a strong sense of 'place' because they led on creating it. The village reflects the quality they designed into it, and its features flow naturally from their thinking and the close relationship they enjoyed with their architect. The village has a strong economic impact on the area. People are coming back to the Vauxhall area to live, and investors also recognize that this is a place with security and a future.

The village is also regarded by outsiders as a desirable place to live. Its success and popularity is such that people from across the city of Liverpool are keen to move there. One resident told me that he enjoys telling Liverpool cab drivers his destination because he always gets a compliment about the village.

So, from a position of imminent demolition and dispersal in the late 1970s, the Eldonians went on to create a community that is recognized by the UN as a World Habitat and meets the criteria for a sustainable community. It is a model inner city neighbourhood that is owned and managed by the people who live in it. They achieved this with the strong leadership of Tony McGann, belief among the people that their cause was just, excellent professional assistance, and a combination of good timing and sheer determination.

Peter Roberts concludes that 'the Eldonian Village offers a practical demonstration of the power of social innovation and community action when it is clearly constructed and well-led'.[12] It is one of longest established examples of community regeneration in the UK, and of this Roberts says:

> The Eldonian Village has taken some twenty years to mature, and this is four times as long as the average lifespan of a community or neighbourhood project. What this suggests is that far more attention than is currently the case needs to be devoted to providing continuity, and to ensuring that effective progression and succession arrangements are put in place at the start of the process of community building.[13]

12 Roberts, 'Social Innovation', 131.

13 Roberts, 'Social Innovation', 132.

The Eldonians are not finished. Most other neighbourhood groups are single issue and stop after they have achieved their goal. After more than twenty-five years the Eldonians continue to push out the boundaries with new ideas for development. Theirs is a 'work in progress'. As George Evans says:

> Sustainability means communities need to keep raising the bar, setting realistic targets then looking to go that little bit further. We have improved housing, health, education, local employment and safety within our community, but there is still a lot more work to be done. Governments for a long time have trusted communities to provide and manage their own housing. Maybe the time has come for them to trust communities to, for example, provide and manage their own health facilities.

These days the Eldonians do not have to lead from the front, as they are active in a variety of partnerships with the public and private sectors. They are keen to see more developments of mixed tenure housing, health facilities and local shops. Their role in partnerships today, however, is that of an investor with a long track record of achievement, not a struggling community fighting for some control over their future.

The Eldonian success story, however, did not happen overnight. It was a long hard struggle, the roots of which lie in the nineteenth century. What follows is an account of their historical background, before we trace their journey to the present day.

The Historical Context

II

THE NEXT THREE chapters introduce the people of Vauxhall, their Church and their housing. We begin in the nineteenth century and end in the 1970s as the people begin their transformation into the Eldonians. This historical perspective is interesting in itself, but the main reason for its inclusion is that the Eldonians themselves believe that it is significant in understanding their story.

Life in Vauxhall: The People

3

THE MAJORITY OF the Eldonians are descended from Irish migrants to Liverpool in the nineteenth century. The Irish potato famine of 1845–47 changed the face of Liverpool. Fleeing poverty and starvation in the south of Ireland, hundreds of thousands of people took the short boat trip from Dublin to Liverpool. The majority continued on to Canada and America, but thousands settled in Liverpool, often due to a lack of money to pay for the onward journey.

This part of the story draws heavily on Robert Scally's *The End of Hidden Ireland*.[1] Scally estimates that between 1847 and 1853, around one million Irish arrived in Liverpool as transients or settlers, of whom some 586,000 were designated as 'paupers' by the authorities. Liverpool's key role was that of a transit camp and depot for goods and people for the New World and beyond.

Scally also reminds us that Liverpool's rise to the position of second city in the UK was founded on the success of its aggressive merchant community in cornering a major share of the trade in slaves, rum, tobacco, sugar, salt and cotton, in addition to its share of Irish provisions. A century and a half later, the last two large industries to close down in the Vauxhall area were the Tate & Lyle sugar refinery and British American Tobacco, both closures having a significant impact on the Eldonians.

Scally writes:

1 Robert Scally, *The End of Hidden Ireland* (Oxford University Press, 1995).

> For the great majority of those leaving all the ports of the inland sea, Liverpool was the almost irresistible magnet whatever their ultimate destination – especially for the superabundant Celtic agrarians uprooted each year with no direction in mind but away from home. Since most of the migrants were general labourers or servants seeking wages in any work that offered itself, they can hardly be said to have destinations in mind before leaving home.[2]

In contrast to the plight of the new arrivals, the owners of the ships, warehouses and goods concerned themselves with serving the ever-growing demand for their wares. This is well illustrated by the amount of investment and planning that went into the infrastructure of the docks and their surrounds compared with the hovels in which many of the dock labourers lived. Throughout the nineteenth century, the Mersey Docks and Harbour Board and its engineers were engaged in a constant development of docks, many of which survive today. Scally writes:

> Of all the public structures in England they were perhaps the frankest symbol of the new empire that had come into being: above all, their purpose was profit and if they exalted any deity it was the Moloch of commerce.[3]

He captures the contrast of this setting for the newly arrived from Ireland:

> Although it had only been a week or less since they had last walked the narrow dirt paths of the townlands, they were now entering a landscape that might have been centuries away. In one of the many startling contrasts that characterised the Liverpool waterfront, its highly rationalised inanimate landscape was peopled to an extraordinary degree by wanderers, casual workers and paupers, most of them recently removed from the land and many of them homeless, squatting among the quays and dock walls oblivious to the purposes of their surroundings.[4]

According to the Vauxhall Society, many of the new arrivals lived in back-to-back slums and cellar dwellings with regular outbreaks of cholera and

2 Scally, *Hidden Ireland*, 192.
3 Scally, *Hidden Ireland*, 198.
4 Scally, *Hidden Ireland*, 199.

An example of the housing used by the new arrivals in Vauxhall at Silvester Street

typhus. In the cholera outbreak in Liverpool in 1849, 2,000 of the recorded 5,000 cholera deaths were in the Vauxhall and Scotland Road area. Those who did not manage to move on to America or Canada, or did not wish to, were unwelcome in the city. The main source of public welfare was the Poor Law Guardians, and they were overwhelmed by the needs of the migrants for housing, health and food.[5]

We get a clear picture of the values of the Poor Law, which came into force on 14 August 1834, from a lecture given by Mike Royden at the Liverpool Medical History/Historic Society of Lancashire and Cheshire Conference in 1999:

> The new Act minimised the provision of outdoor relief and made confinement in a workhouse the central element of the new system. To qualify… they actually had to be destitute. Only the truly deserving – in the opinion of the government – would be those 'desiring' to reside in such a repellent institution. To help them in their decision, the

5 The Vauxhall Society, www.vauxhallsociety.org.uk, 2005.

> surroundings were made as unpleasant as possible as an obvious deterrent to those seeking relief.[6]

Finally, Scally helps us understand another aspect of the desperate plight of the Irish arrivals in the middle of the nineteenth century in Liverpool:

> Liverpool's casual tolerance of suffering had had generations of breeding in the slave trade and the trekking of destitute agrarians from the poorest parts of the kingdom. A majority of its population in 1848 was constituted by these earlier immigrants: Scots, Ulstermen, Welsh and Irish who had come as manual labourers and occupied the congested slum wards into which the new migrants were now crowding. In no other place were these factious Celtic elements brought together in such numbers and intimacy. Contact between them was accompanied by a level of violence higher than anywhere else.[7]

The majority of the mid-nineteenth-century arrivals were Catholic and they settled in the Vauxhall area of the city, probably because it is within walking distance of Liverpool's Pier Head. One of the many impacts of their arrival was on the role of the Catholic Church in the city at that time.

Jim Dunne was parish priest at Our Lady's parish in Vauxhall for nineteen years, spanning the emergence of the Eldonians as a force to be reckoned with. At the time he was Monsignor Dunne, a man of some considerable influence on the fate of the Eldonians, as we shall hear later. He comments on the Catholic Church in the nineteenth century:

> When you think of the Catholic Church in the north west, and in particular the Archdiocese of Liverpool, then you have to make a distinction between Catholic Lancashire – places like Chorley and Wigan – and the city of Liverpool. There were vast differences between these two. Catholic Lancashire had retained, more than any other place in the country, the old religion if I could call it that, in the days when the rest of the country was rapidly becoming transformed into the Anglican Church in its spiritual direction.

6 Mike W. Royden, 'The 19th Century Poor Law in Liverpool and its Hinterland: Towards the Origins of the Workhouse Infirmary', lecture given at the Liverpool Medical History/Historic Society of Lancashire and Cheshire Conference 'The Poor Law and After: Workhouse Hospitals and Public Welfare', 10 April 1999.

7 Scally, *Hidden Ireland*, 211.

In fact, the Catholics in the early part of nineteenth century had no churches in this part of Liverpool, while there were a number of redundant Anglican churches. In 1847 the Vicar Apostolic (the Catholic vicar in charge of the area at that time) bought St Anne's church from the Anglicans, and renamed it St Joseph's, one of the earliest churches in Scotland Road.

Jim Dunne continues:

> Liverpool, having been invaded, so to speak, by the Irish after the famine in 1847, experienced a *tremendous* transformation. And what happened was that they settled all along the docks and drove the Protestants up the hill, and that created, I think, a great resentment. The Irish that arrived in the city were illiterate, vermin-ridden, starving and had no priests. It took some time – about thirty years – before priests began to come in any numbers, and they were from Ireland. And they tended to be middle-class as opposed to the immigrants who had been from agricultural parts of Ireland.

So, the start of life in England for the Eldonians ancestors' was not promising. The next significant factor to consider is the role of the Church in their lives.

4 Life in Vauxhall: The Church

The effect of the great influx of Irish Catholics was to turn the Vauxhall area from Protestant to mainly Catholic in a short number of years. So what role did the Church play from that time until the 1970s?

According to Jim Dunne, the Catholic Church in the nineteenth century had a committed and parochial following in Vauxhall:

> In the days of the new St Joseph's in 1877 the population of each parish would have been about 9,000 each, so you can do the multiplication. In fact there's a record from about the early part of the twentieth century where there was a very irate letter written by the parish priest of St Joseph's to the Bishop referring to his proposal to make a new parish (Holy Cross) by cutting off 6,000 people from St Joseph's: that would leave him with only 19,000 parishioners!

The church was also wealthy – the contrast between the living conditions of the priest and his parishioners being very stark. Jim Dunne found it curious that the newly arrived Irish did not appear to object to the rather splendid conditions in which the Catholic priests lived compared to their own squalid conditions. He concluded:

> Why was there no anti-clericalism? My reason for the question was in France, for example, there was rabid anti-clericalism at the time of the revolution. In England and in Liverpool there was no anti-clericalism to talk about. When they built the new St Joseph's in 1877, they built

a presbytery that housed four priests and four servants and was five floors. Every fitting in the house was brass; every piece of wood in the doors and skirting boards was pine. The rooms had high ceilings; it was very spacious and solidly built.

Across the street, within yards of that building, there was a Court, as they were called, where the people lived, and these were old terraced houses, facing each other with no indoor toilets, no indoor water. The water was obtained from a pump that supplied them with cold water.

And the question I asked myself was: why was there not resentment towards these priests living in such a different style? And my answer to that is: well, it takes two to make a deal, and some deal had been struck between the people and the clergy. And the deal was this: they needed people to be out of the shit, who would absolve them and when it came to die, would administer the last rites to them. And if you want to know why the last rites were so important to these people you have to go back in history almost to the middle ages or before the middle ages, when to die without absolution was a tragic, tragic happening for people. And

The type of courts that Jim Dunne describes

> that had lingered on so that the priest represented absolution; he represented a gate to heaven. They didn't *want* him to be in poverty and so on, so they accepted that this was right for the clergy. I defy anyone to give me a better explanation than that.

Talking of his own time as a priest in Vauxhall, around a century later, Jim Dunne confirms that little had changed in terms of the dominance of the Catholic Church in the area; it was an 'extraordinarily homogeneous community':

> The area remained totally Catholic, with a few exceptions, so much so that if a Missioner came – as they did every few years to liven up the parish and give them a bit of a jolt – and wanted to visit the Catholics in the parish, in *that* area in Scotland Road the parish priest would simply hand him a list of *streets* – not a list of addresses – and say 'that's what the parish consists of; visit everybody there'.

Another characteristic was the compactness of each parish, and the compactness of the area. In 1976, when Jim Dunne became priest at St Joseph's:

> If you put a pin in a map in the mother church, St Anthony's, in Scotland Road, and took just half a mile diameter and drew a circle so that nobody in that half mile diameter would be more than half a mile from the Church, you would enclose something like fifteen or sixteen parishes within that half mile.

How, then, was this large and expensive edifice financed? By assiduous collecting from the people, according to Jim Dunne. He remembers in the 1960s, for example, when he was curate in St Sylvester's parish, the priest used to go to a different section of the parish regularly, so that the parish would be covered every two or three weeks. He would be preceded by a person, a child maybe, who would knock on the door and would say 'Father Dunne please', and the priest would find the door open. When he arrived, he would walk straight in, with a bag in his hand, would exchange a couple of pleasantries with the people and they would put some money in the bag. The weeks when the priests didn't call, a lay person would be appointed to call instead. Jim recalls that the laymen, however, would not get as much as the priest!

There was no escape from this 'Catholic tax', as Jim Dunne called it, as he too was obliged to raise revenue in this way once he was the parish priest in Vauxhall in the 1970s:

> I've often gone into a pub in Scotland Road and shouted 'St Joseph's please', and some of the guys who were propping up the bar would have ill-concealed resentment as they put their hands in their pockets when the priest dangled the bag in front of their noses!

This is something that local people who grew up in the Vauxhall area remember. Rita Potter and Peggy Hackett are both in their late sixties and still live in the area. They remarked that these contributions were in addition to the weekly collections in church and in the Catholic schools. This practice of local contributions to the Church was to influence these people's emergence as a fighting community, as we shall see later – they believed that they owned the Church's buildings:

> He'd come around and the altar boy used to knock on the door 'the priest is coming'. They'd have the money ready. Even if families were *skint*, they'd give the priest a half-a-crown. My ninny [grandmother] did, on a Sunday afternoon. So all our money built them churches, built the priest's house. (Rita)

So, to summarize, the Catholic Church was central to the community from the arrival of the Irish migrants to the early 1980s. First, it was important for people to worship and to receive the various 'sacraments' of the Church. Secondly, people wanted the priest in his role as their pastor. And finally, they had pride in the large church building and the priest's house that they paid for, as Rita Potter told us, albeit begrudgingly.

The Catholic Church in the 1970s

By the 1970s a new role for the local parish priest was slowly emerging. It was the new generation of priests who developed this role, and their motive was concern for the issues facing the people who lived in their parish. This was a worldwide trend in the Catholic Church during this period. It became known as 'Liberation Theology' and was particularly effective in parts of the world run by repressive regimes, such as in parts of South America.

Jim Dunne, the parish priest for the Eldonians from the mid-1970s, and his fellow priest, Michael Lane, were of the new generation of priests. They both had a commitment to improving the living conditions of the people of their parish, and both were catalysts in developing the skills and confidence of the people who went on to become the Eldonians.

Unlike his fellow priests, Jim had grown up in the Victoria Square tenements, which were adjacent to the Vauxhall area, and so he had first-hand experience of what life was like and of the issues facing people who were living in poverty. So, when he returned to the area in the early 1960s, following training for the priesthood and social work, this time as a young curate, he came with a perspective that went well beyond the 'spiritual'. He says, 'I don't think that they experienced me as being typical of the priests. And in fact I'm quite certain that I wasn't typical.'

As he visited his parishioners, he would hear about a son being out of work or a husband being sick, and he began to pick up a chorus of references to what they called 'the Welfare'. He knew they were talking about the Children's Department or Probation Department or the Unemployment Bureau. What irked him was that they assumed that he would have no interest in their problems of sickness, unemployment, bad housing or whatever. They did not see that as his business. What they saw as his business was administering to their 'spiritual' needs and raising money to build a Catholic school.

After many years in social work for the Archdiocese, Jim Dunne again returned to Vauxhall in the mid-1970s, just as Tony McGann was emerging as the natural leader and community activist among the people living in the tenements in Jim's parish. Tony recalls that both Jim Dunne and Michael Lane were 'community minded', and they had a profound effect on his understanding and respect for the role of the Church. He recalls Jim telling him about a visit to Gerard Gardens in St Joseph's parish:

> I [Jim Dunne] was standing on the fourth or fifth landing, having walked up flights of stairs strewn with broken glass, smelling of urine and with walls covered with graffiti, and looking down at the square with broken flagstones, litter and broken swings. I asked myself the question 'is this shit God's Kingdom?' And the answer was 'yes'.

Tony's admiration for Jim stems from this approach. He recalls Jim saying about his role as a priest: 'You've got to get involved in the communities; it's not just about saying mass on Sunday. People are living in these conditions; you've got to get out there and do something.' Tony added: 'I learnt an awful lot from Jim Dunne and Michael Lane – even though we did not always agree with each other – because I could see where they were coming from.' He remembers their message to him: 'Go out there and make things happen. You're doing God's work by making a difference to people's lives for the better.'

While most of the people of Vauxhall were always committed Catholics; in the 1970s they and their leader, Tony McGann, learnt a great deal from their new-style priests. In Jim Dunne and Michael Lane they had the additional benefit of two men who understood the social problems of the area and 'stood up' alongside their parishioners when it mattered. The 'social agenda' of the two priests was to be an important factor in the emergence of this new community group.

In the next chapter, we look at the final significant historical factor for the Eldonians – their housing.

5 Life in Vauxhall: The Housing

The area where most of the early Irish migrants settled was along the docks to the north of the city centre, including Vauxhall, within walking distance of the Pier Head and adjacent to the main source of casual work. The main type of housing in which they lived in those early days was purpose-built court housing, constructed by speculative builders. These dwellings were popular among builders because they were cheap and easy to construct and they had the minimum of standards and facilities.

How did the descendants of these first immigrants end up living in tenements over a century later? John Tarn, in his book *Five Per Cent Philanthropy*,[1] provides some answers to this question. Tarn was Professor of Architecture at the University of Liverpool and worked there from 1974 to 1999, writing extensively about the history of both housing and architecture. Tarn helps us to understand the background to the tenements, which were built mainly in poor working-class areas in most towns and cities in the UK, and were the main type of housing in Vauxhall up to the time of the Eldonians.

The first significant development in addressing the appalling housing conditions of the urban poor came in 1843, when the government set up a Royal Commission on the health of towns. The final report came out in 1845 and Tarn explains its profound impact:

1 John Tarn, *Five Per Cent Philanthropy: An Account of Housing in Urban Areas between 1840 and 1914* (Cambridge University Press, 1973).

Another example of the old courts that preceded the tenements in the 1930s

> By 1845... the whole sordid story of the growth of industrial England had been exposed and committed to cold print in the pages of parliamentary papers, for all who cared to read them. They made a massive and revolting indictment of the *laissez faire* philosophers of the older generation. But it took many years for the evils of health and housing to be rectified and it required the reversal of many prized social theories. It was one thing to expose the evils of existing towns; it was quite another to cure them.[2]

Following this report, the foundations of the model housing movement were laid, with a growing understanding that the community as a whole could help the working classes by supporting the construction of model dwellings, which were subsequently carefully managed.

In 1848 the first Public Health Act was passed by Parliament, the culmination of the change from *laissez faire* to public responsibility. Local Public Health Boards were created, with powers to insist on adequate drainage, sanitary accommodation, water supply and sewers for new housing. They also

2 Tarn, *Five Per Cent Philanthropy*, 3.

St Martin's Cottages in Vauxhall: The first municipal housing built in provincial England, completed in 1869

empowered local authorities to levy a rate for these services.[3] In Liverpool the local authority instructed the Borough Engineer to identify sites owned by the Corporation suitable for new rented accommodation. The main site was at Ashfield Street in Vauxhall. Private builders were invited to submit designs, but in the event none did, so the Corporation borrowed money for construction from the Public Works Loan Commission. Thus were St Martin's Cottages completed in 1869, the first municipal housing to be built in provincial England.

Although these were rather bleak in appearance and close together, they were a step in the right direction in Tarn's opinion. They broke the long-held view that housing was the domain of the private speculator, and thus a sense of civic responsibility took root in Liverpool. In fact, Tarn tells us that the review of St Martin's Cottages in *The Builder* magazine at the time recommended that those who built for the poor should 'mix a little philanthropy with their percentage calculations'.[4]

Some eighteen months later another 132 tenements were built behind St Martin's Cottages, called Ashfield Cottages. This led to the third development, which was more carefully designed – Victoria Square at Juvenal Street,

3 Tarn, *Five Per Cent Philanthropy*, 9.

4 Tarn, *Five Per Cent Philanthropy*, 62.

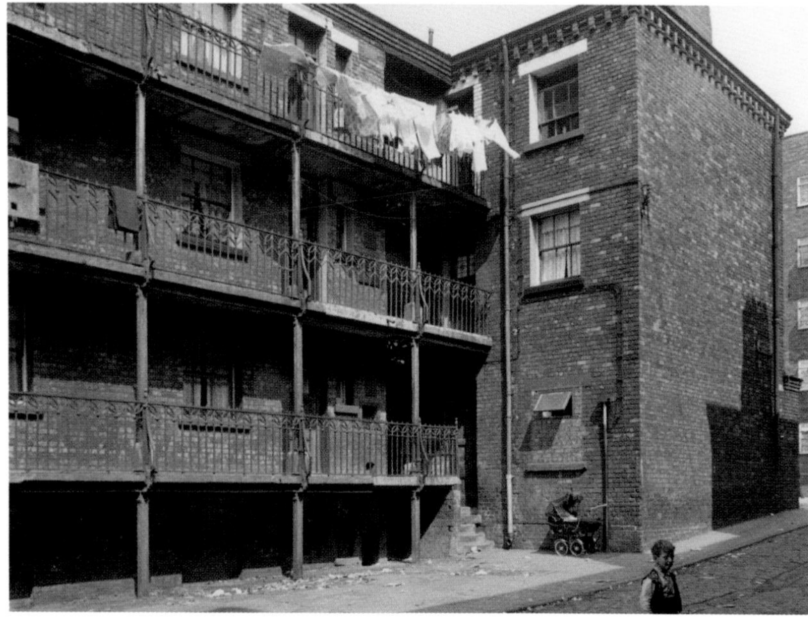

Ashfield Cottages: Built in 1871, also in Vauxhall, and demolished along with St Martin's Cottages in the 1960s

adjacent to Vauxhall, opened in 1885. The Victoria Square development was an important milestone for the future development of the Vauxhall tenements in the 1930s. *The Builder* magazine of 1886 stated:

> In judging the financial result of the scheme it has to be borne in mind that the object of the Corporation was not to cover this site to its full capacity with dwellings, but to erect buildings of the best class for their purpose and of the highest sanitary standard, thus affording an example to be followed in the future by private enterprise, while at the same time, providing a large unbuilt-upon space in this densely-populated district.[5]

It was here, at Victoria Square, that Jim Dunne was raised by his aunt Martha from the age of two until he was twenty-four. He has only good memories of living there, and recalls a saying when he was a child: 'You have to have a letter from the Holy Ghost to get in!'

St Martin's Cottages, Ashfield Cottages and Victoria Square were all demolished in the 1960s. The demolition of Victoria Square in 1966 made way for the new tunnel under the River Mersey, and the area where it was located is today a grim combination of dense new houses living cheek by jowl with the Mersey Tunnel.

5 Tarn, *Five Per Cent Philanthropy*, 91.

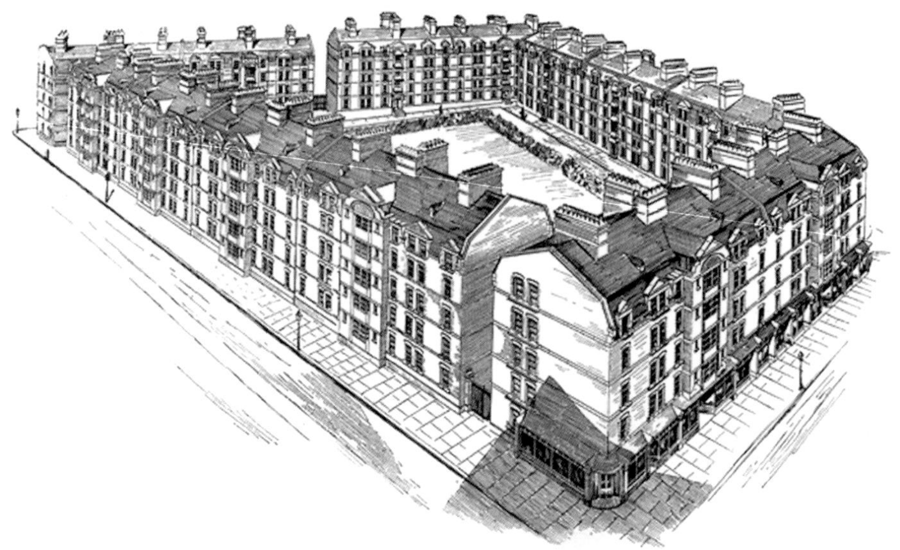

The Victoria Square tenements built in 1885, where Jim Dunne was raised by his Aunt Martha

The next major landmark in the development of public housing was the Public Health Act of 1875, which was of particular interest to the people living in slums in the Vauxhall area. For the first time, the local authority was vested with wide-ranging powers of enforcement governing sewers and their maintenance, street cleaning, water supplies and building regulations including space and sanitary standards. Significantly for Vauxhall, no new cellar dwellings were to be permitted, and those already in use were allowed to continue only if they met new standards.

The last major foundation stone of government legislation that paved the way for state intervention in the provision of healthy, well-designed housing was the Housing of the Working Classes Act of 1890. Tarn argues: 'This piece of legislation swept away the age of self interest, the microcosmic reactionary housing institutions, and heralded the arrival of new civic authorities, based, at least in part, in a democratic framework, that were anxious to sweep away the cobwebs of Victorian philanthropy'.[6] The Act gave local authorities the powers they needed to plan programmes of slum clearance, including compulsory purchase, and to plan new neighbourhoods with streets and sewers. This was to be the start of the cycle of slum clearance programmes in Liverpool, one of which triggered the Eldonian story, as will be explained later.

6 Tarn, *Five Per Cent Philanthropy*, 123.

The final piece in our jigsaw tracing the origins of the tenements in Liverpool concerns Sir Lancelot Keay. Keay was born in Sussex in 1883, trained as an architect and was appointed as Liverpool City Architect and Director of Housing in 1925. His primary responsibility in these early years was planning and overseeing the large slum clearance programme in the city. During his time in Liverpool, more than 35,000 houses were built, including the township of Speke. Keay retired in 1948. John Belchem claims that when it came to tackling slum clearance, Liverpool Corporation was 'the most progressive authority in the field'.[7]

Keay faced the need for a slum clearance programme in the heavily populated city centre and in the dock areas, from the Dingle in the south end of the city through to Vauxhall in the north. Given the success of tenements in Liverpool before his time, particularly Victoria Square, he must have recognized that this was the way to deal with the issue of the town centre and the docks areas. Ged Fagan, who has written excellent books on life in the Gerard Gardens tenements in the city centre, says that in the 1930s Keay took a delegation of colleagues to visit the city of Vienna in Austria, and that this trip provided him and his team with inspiration on how to tackle the problems back in Liverpool.[8]

For the Social Democratic local authority of Vienna in the 1920s and 1930s, the tenement design expressed its socialist ideals. It included new facilities for health, education and culture, internal toilets and cold water, balconies and courtyard access to the flats rather than access from the street. It assumed that the balconies and courtyard access would encourage more contact between neighbours, as well as allowing residents to watch out for each other.

The inspiration from Vienna could be seen in the design and layout of many of the tenements built in Liverpool in the 1930s, particularly Gerard Gardens, St Andrew's Gardens and Portland Gardens. As in Vienna, the new tenements in Liverpool were intended to foster a sense of 'community' and to this end they were all called 'Gardens' because the buildings were constructed around a central courtyard or 'garden'. The courtyard was intended to be a communal play and meeting area, with people's front doors opening onto a deck that overlooked it. Each of the tenements had resident managers and caretakers, who were not replaced after the Second World War. In fact the

7 John Belchem, 'Celebrating Liverpool', in John Belchem (ed.), *Liverpool 800: Culture, Character and History* (Liverpool University Press, 2006), 20.

8 Ged Fagan, *Liverpool In A City Living* (Countyvise Limited, 2004).

central courtyards were turned into shelters during the war and were never reinstated, and soon became bleak tarmac areas.

Although most of these tenements are now gone, they were an important part of urban life in Liverpool. They worked for the people who lived in them from the late 1930s to their demolition, mainly in the 1970s and 80s. Communities were created and grew up in them and the people of Vauxhall were no exception. The next section will explore why people came to be very attached to these tenements, and how they contributed to the development of a sense of community among the residents.

Why did the Vauxhall tenements work?

I spoke at some length with people in Vauxhall who grew up in tenements and they all described how much they loved living in them. They present a wonderful picture of how the buildings and courtyards worked for those who lived there. Their memories and stories also provide us with the first and most powerful explanation for their eventual resistance to Liverpool City Council's plans to demolish their tenements, namely their strong sense of belonging here.

The remainder of this chapter contains the testimonies of Rita Potter, Eileen O'Brien, Peggy Hackett, Lilian Grimes, John Livingston and Joan McGann, all in their sixties, who grew up in the tenements in and around Vauxhall; also the testimony of Margaret Dragonette, who is in her forties, who was born and raised in the Eldon Street tenements and is now employed by the Eldonian CBHA. They talk about their lives as young adults and parents in the 1950s and 1960s, when the flats were in a fairly good condition and were generally clean and tidy.

They spoke first about the mutual trust among neighbours:

> ... it was good, the community, everybody helped everybody else... Everybody knocked on everybody's door. If anyone was sick, a neighbour would say 'I'm going to the wash house now, give us all your washing' – that same person could have seven or eight kids of their own but still take all your washing to the wash house for you. Another one would go and do all your shopping, come in and have a meal ready for the kids coming home from school and your husband coming home from work.
>
> The neighbours were excellent, just excellent. *Everybody* helped

Gerard Gardens: the design was inspired by the Marxist architecture of Vienna

Gerard Gardens: The main entrance to the tenements

St Andrews Gardens: tenements from the 1930s with the familiar decks

A rear view of Portland Gardens towards the end of its life in the 1980s

> everybody else. And different people got paid different days, so some got paid on a Thursday, so you could go and borrow ten shilling off the woman next door and pay her back on the Thursday. You'd even lend your Family Allowance on Sunday afternoon and you'd get it back on Thursday afternoon! (Rita Potter)

Peggy Hackett further describes this 'mutual aid':

> It was lovely; we had plenty of nice friends and neighbours, very helpful, lovely neighbours who would give before you asked them. Mrs B. used to say 'If you need anything, just come and ask me'. She had 17 children, and when I went into hospital to have my first baby she said 'No matter what time it is, I'm coming with you' and she did... When someone was skint and said I've only got two bob, we'd go to the 10 o'clock shop in Lewis Street off Scotland Road and get a little bag of tea, two ounces of tea and half a pound of sugar... and you helped one another. You'd go to the pawn shop for them, and go back on a Friday and get it out for them.

Joan McGann, Tony's wife, also grew up in these tenements and she recalls their neighbourliness: 'The neighbours were great; there'd be arguments but a few days after they'd stand and talk so it wasn't carried on'. Asked why she thought people related to each other in this way, she said:

> I think that people then had been brought up with a different way of life. They'd been through a war and everything else, they'd been through all that, and they just seemed to get on better together. There was no competition then; everybody was equal and everyone was in the same boat.

How tidy and safe was the environment for play? Looking back further to her own childhood, Peggy says:

> Oh it was safe, you could go anywhere for hours and hours. No-one would bother you. You'd play out in the square for hours; we used to play lally-oh up the landings and down the other side. We had a bike shelter like a garage, and we used to all play on top of that. No-one bothered you.

Margaret recalled how they 'used local resources': 'We used to have a little bonfire in the street and we'd get pans and wash the pans out and get sugar and make our own toffee – go down to Tate & Lyle and take some sugar!'

As mentioned above, the architects who designed the tenements to include central courts and decks intended them to add to the sense of safety and community. This is borne out in the memories of these Eldonians. Peggy provides us with a description of how both these features worked for the residents:

> The children would play in the square, as we called it, and people were always on the landings watching, because they'd come out to empty something – the chutes were on the landing to put your rubbish down. So you'd come out to do that and stand there, and Rita'd come out and you'd stand talking to her, and it was like that all day and night… always someone on the landing watching them.

Why was it that people cared for each other and acted as good neighbours? Eileen O'Brien suggests:

> I think it was the people themselves, the people who came to live in this part. I think they came from different backgrounds, maybe it was the Irish famine and the Welsh and different things, and people just more or less had to get on. It's just like everything else – when you started from nothing, you only built up. I think those people were the foundation, but they all built on it, they wanted it a little bit better. They never had many luxuries, as you know, because it was hard going.

Lilian Grimes concludes: 'but nobody complained'. Eileen offers a final word: 'No, you just accepted it, but you moved on and you've got to move on.' This final thought, in many ways, reflects the fundamental spirit of the Eldonians who, thirty years later, are still moving on!

By the 1970s the tenements in the Vauxhall area were in a very poor state of repair. The public areas were dirty and neglected, with graffiti and litter everywhere. The general appearance was one of abandonment and despair. The photographs from that time clearly illustrate this. But still, the sense of community was strong. George Evans, now the Eldonians' Director of Housing, but then a young council Housing Officer, described the early morning scene in a tenement courtyard as 'a dawn chorus' of people chatting

Life on the decks: The Burlington Street tenements in the mid-1980s

The grim environment of Burlington Street in the 1980s; Portland Gardens is on the left

The 'playground' on Burlington Street

and calling to each other across the decks. And despite these conditions, the people who lived here did not want to live in any other part of the city. As Margaret Dragonette says, 'I've only ever known Eldon Street and Burlington Street; I've never lived anywhere else, never *wanted* to live anywhere else.'

Conclusion

Over the last three chapters, we have looked at the people of Vauxhall, their Church and their housing. The people who eventually became known as the Eldonians are descended from people who arrived in Liverpool in total poverty and who were not made welcome. They were people who most likely had to fight for their most basic needs such as food, work, housing and care. They grew to realize they had to 'defend their corner'. They would have known that they could not return to Ireland or go on to Canada or America.

They initially made their homes in the cellar houses of the badly built court houses that littered the area along the docks. Amidst this scene of deprivation and despair, the Catholic Church slowly began to grow, and offered one of the few clean and respectable places where people felt welcome. It is no wonder then that the Church became one of the 'pillars' of their society – it offered refuge and, as Jim Dunne told us, it offered absolution on their death beds.

From the outset, local people contributed on a regular basis to the establishment and upkeep of all the Catholic buildings and the priests who lived in

Perhaps the young boy at the top is telling us that 'it's thumbs up for the people and thumbs down for the place'.

them. It is no wonder then that people felt they 'owned every brick in all the buildings'. Latterly, however, the Church also provided its parishioners with leadership skills. The priests in the 1970s and 1980s were aware of the social issues facing the people of Vauxhall and were also willing to help them to do something about these issues. In particular, they wanted to work alongside local leaders to tackle the problems of poor housing, the lack of local facilities and the poor environment. They were the first role models for Tony McGann, the Eldonians' leader, who was very keen to learn.

The new tenements in the 1930s succeeded in fostering a sense of community. We have heard from a number of people who grew up in them and confirmed that the design worked, in that they all felt a sense of comradeship or community, or as Joan McGann said, 'everybody was equal and everyone was in the same boat'. Seventy years of living in these tenements produced a very strong sense of place, of community, of belonging. Despite their gradual decline and deterioration, these important characteristics remained, and the residents would fight to retain them.

The Eldonians inherited from their ancestors the tradition of defending their place when external pressures threatened it. This characteristic, along with their 'ownership' of their churches and the encouragement offered by their priests, combined to set the scene for the next phase of their story – namely, their resistance to the Archdiocese of Liverpool's decision to rationalize the Vauxhall parishes, and the decision of Liverpool City Council to demolish their tenements and disperse the inhabitants throughout the city.

The Eldonians' Journey

We have looked at the Eldonian Village as it is today, and at the history of the people and place of Vauxhall. Now we begin to trace the events between 1976 and 1987, which led to this particular group of people becoming 'The Eldonians'. This was the most formative period in the Eldonians' history and resulted in the establishment of the Eldonian Village. While the village continues to develop today, it was during these years that the people of Vauxhall fought and won the key battles that ensured its creation and ongoing success.

This section of the book begins with their first campaign, which was against the Catholic Church, aided by the people's local parish priests. It culminates in their victory over Liverpool City Council, when they appealed and won a Planning Inquiry to re-designate an industrial site – the former Tate & Lyle refinery – to housing use. Along the way they made many friends with their courage and determination to do what was right for them. These included Secretaries of State, Chief Executives, Bishops and Archbishops, and other groups in Liverpool who watched their brave struggle from a distance.

The Archdiocese Campaign

6

In February 1976 Derek Worlock was appointed Archbishop of Liverpool. He came with a commitment both to understand the issues facing people living in deprived inner city areas, and to reorganize the diocese, because there were too many churches and not enough churchgoers. He quickly set about his challenge of reorganization, which included the parishes in Vauxhall. At this time the Catholic Church still had a significant impact on the lives of most of the people living in this part of the city. It followed, therefore, that any plan to rationalize the number of churches was bound to have repercussions for parishioners living there. And it did!

This plan by the Archdiocese was to be the cause of the first campaign among local people to organize against an external threat to their way of life. There had been other threats, such as the construction of the new Mersey Tunnel that went through the middle of their neighbourhood in the early 1970s, and the gradual closure of the docks as trade shifted to the east and south coasts. These had major negative impacts on local people but were, they felt, beyond the influence of community action

There were eleven parishes in Vauxhall and, despite the relatively small geographical area, people felt a strong allegiance to their particular parish. As Tony McGann said, 'there were all different parishes round here, and if you lived in the next street, you lived a million miles away, that's how parochial people were'. These allegiances, however, would be set aside for the purposes of joint action to save all the parish churches and retain their local priests.

This campaign did not lead directly to the development of the Eldonian

Village, but it was important in the development of the community. First, it galvanized local people around an issue that they felt strongly about and believed they could influence. Secondly, it was through this campaign that Tony McGann emerged as a leader. His leadership then, and up to the present day, is key to understanding the Eldonian story and all that they have achieved.

The Archbishop appointed Jim Dunne to lead a team of priests and sisters to take an interest in the area's social problems, and to implement his plan to rationalize the structure of parishes. The plan was based on a study he had made of the Archdiocese when he first arrived. For the Vauxhall area he had decided to amalgamate the existing eleven parishes. Their boundaries would be abolished and they would become one unit under a Dean.

At this time Jim Dunne was Monsignor James Dunne, the Vicar General and 'the Archbishop's man'. Both Jim Dunne and Tony McGann recall the dissatisfaction of the various parish priests with the Archbishop's plans. Indeed Tony recalls being approached by Dean O'Connell, his own parish priest at Our Lady's, and Father O'Riley from St Anthony's on Scotland Road, who 'briefed me about having to set up a campaign against the Archbishop'. So, with the blessing of local priests, he went out on his first organizing campaign, the first of many! He went to all eleven parishes, talking to people, and agreeing that they should express their disapproval at a meeting called by the Archdiocese.

Jim Dunne recalls, with some amusement, that public meeting:

> The mistake he [the Archbishop] made was that when he spoke to the 200 or so parishioners, he addressed them from the stage, and behind him he had ranged the parish priests of the parishes in question, including myself. As he explained his intentions to abolish the parish boundaries, the priests behind him indicated their displeasure by simply shaking their heads. And that gave a signal to the people in the audience!

The audience took their cue from this clear sign and began to shout 'No! We want to keep our parishes', with Tony McGann taking a lead in this, shaking his fists, half-standing, as he shouted 'No, No, No!'

So what did Jim Dunne think of the reaction of Tony McGann and his neighbours to these plans of the newly arrived Archbishop? It was predictable, he thinks, as they resented the idea of being asked to do anything differently. The meeting ended with a great deal of bad feeling and with the Archbishop standing his ground. However, after the meeting, he decided not to proceed with the plan, but he asked Jim Dunne to go to Vauxhall anyway and to help people not only spiritually but also with their social problems.

A decade later, Archbishop Worlock reflected on this resistance to his plans:

> One of the strongest impressions I received on coming to Liverpool from the south was that the intense loyalty of northern Catholics was directed primarily to externals, such as 'our' parish, 'our' priest, 'our' archbishop and even 'our' social club. This was not always a blind thing, but it did not imply much understanding of underlying belief. Resistance to change was probably tougher about the threatened closure of a presbytery in a depopulated area than it would be about some new insights into the nature of the Church's mission. It also meant that if the externals were changed, as when people were uprooted to new estates where church, priest and fellow parishioners were different, believing could cease when there was no longer a sense of belonging.[1]

In November 1976 Jim Dunne returned to the neighbourhoods of his childhood, became the priest at St Joseph's in Vauxhall, and began his journey with the Eldonians. He was relieved that the plan was abandoned,

> ... because by that time I thought 'this is a mistake'. I had a feeling that we were talking about a series of villages here; we were not talking about people who could relate in a really good way to the people in the next neighbourhood or parish. I knew from my own experience that the church in each neighbourhood was its focal point. The people had gone to the parish schools, infants, juniors and seniors – this was before the comprehensives. So, at that time, they had no knowledge of mixing with people from other parishes.

He also recalls the deep suspicion of 'outsiders'. When he first went into the local school to talk about the community, its social problems and its needs, he was attacked by the headmaster, who asked him 'What do *you* know about this area anyway?' Fortunately, he was able to reply: 'Well, first of all I was brought up in it [Victoria Square]. I was an altar boy in it, I've been a curate in it, and I'm *back* in it now as the parish priest!'

1 David Sheppard and Derek Worlock, *Better Together* (Hodder & Stoughton, 1988), 57.

What did Jim think that the people living in the Eldon Street area, particularly Tony McGann, learnt from the experience of taking on and 'beating' the Archdiocese?

> I think it was a very helpful experience, because they took on the Archdiocese and made it back down, and that must have been a reassurance to them that if they stuck together they could beat the authorities. It was interesting, this word 'authorities' was very often trotted out – it could be the government, the local council, or it could be the diocese – when 'the authorities' said something, the people were expected to shut up. Whereas now, I think, they were saying: 'Wait a minute – who do you mean, authorities?' I think it was a shot in the arm.

This episode was to be a capacity building milestone, particularly for Tony. It helped him to recognize his standing with his neighbours, and the influence that he could bring to bear on situations. These insights were to have an impact on him for the next thirty years. Looking back on why he was the one who became the organizer, who stood up at the meeting to express strongly the sentiments of his neighbours, Tony says 'I never wanted to be a leader; I just wanted to keep our church at the time. I think nobody else wanted to do it, I was shoved to the front.'

Tony believes that it was this event that started the ball rolling for him. Shortly after the climb-down by the Archbishop, Tony became involved in the Catholic Men's Society. He was having a pint in the pub one night and the phone rang. It was Dean O'Connell, his parish priest, who wanted to meet with him:

> I went along, and it was to meet local businessmen, which was unheard of back then. He asked me to be a governor on Our Lady's School. Because he was putting me there, he must have had some faith in me… I think he was saying to me, 'I'm putting you in there before I go because I know you'll carry the fight on' – keeping the churches open and everything else.

He also recalls the reaction of some of his neighbours to his unusual appointment: 'a lot of people said, "Hang on, what's he doing as a governor, he used to play billiards with me" and all this. So, I was a governor of the school, a first in this area.'

This was a critical moment for local residents and for Tony McGann's 'sense of self'. Through local organizing and the support of the local priests, they had achieved their first 'victory' as a community; and they had gained confidence in the fight. It was to serve them well in the very near future. It also united the local people and their Church, so that they would stand together when it came time to resist the city council and their plans for demolishing the neighbourhood. Tony sums up this outcome as, 'God works in mysterious ways.'

Before moving on to the next development of the story, Chapter 7 provides a short biography of Tony McGann, the figure who was now emerging as the leader, and illustrates the extent to which his neighbours came to depend on him.

7 'What are you going to do about these earthquakes, Tony?'

By 1976 Tony McGann was recognized as the person to whom other people turned for leadership, advice and support. As he says in the previous chapter, he did not go looking for this role and it was not an official position, at least not yet. This new role was one that was accepted by his neighbours and by the official 'leaders' of the community including the priests, the school principals and the main local councillor, Paul Orr, of whom we will hear later.

Tony was born in 1937 in Gildarts Gardens in the Vauxhall area. These were old 'court style' dwellings built in 1897. He was raised with his nine brothers and sisters by his mother and stepfather, who did casual work on the docks and therefore brought little money into the house. He says:

> We lived in sheer poverty. I don't know how my mother and all those other people who lived round this area survived, mainly because you wouldn't know where the next meal was coming from. You'd go to school, and half the time you wouldn't have a breakfast because there was no money. You'd come home and you'd have a meal, which your mother had there – I don't know how she managed to get it.

He described how Jewish traders provided some relief for many of the families living in this poverty. 'If it was not for these Jewish tradesmen, we often would not have had meals.' Each week clothing traders would come out from the centre of the city to the people living in Vauxhall. They issued tickets for clothes, shoes and other goods, for which people paid a small amount each week:

Gildarts Gardens where Tony McGann was born and grew up, which was demolished in 1971 to make way for the second Mersey Tunnel

> And what you did was, once you had a suit and shoes, on the Monday morning you took them to a pawn shop, to pawn them to get money for meals for during the week. You had collateral, and if it wasn't for that happening we would have gone without food.

When Tony was fifteen years old, he finished school on a Friday morning, 12 o'clock. His mother then marched him over to a nearby factory, where he started work at 1 o'clock. Tony recalls 'She'd already been into the boss and he said "as soon as he finishes". I think he meant Monday, but she sent me over on the Friday afternoon as soon as I'd finished!' Eventually, he found work at another factory in the neighbourhood and worked there for twenty-two years, mainly as a fork-lift driver.

While still living in Gildarts Gardens with his family, Tony had his first experience of the devastation of a community, which happened, as far as he can recall, without any consultation or public meetings. This was the construction of the new Mersey Tunnel to provide more access to and from the Wirral and Liverpool. It was commissioned by Merseyside County Council (since

The construction of the tunnel meant the destruction of long-standing communities and the loss of hundreds of local jobs.

abolished). Work commenced in 1968 and it was completed in 1971. In this area that had survived the extensive bombing of Liverpool in the Second World War, everything was demolished, including some 500 houses built only five years before. He remembers:

> People were rehoused to Speke and Skelmersdale [on the outskirts of Liverpool] and the old community was broken up. I heard of old people who died of a broken heart because they were just shipped out... The jobs and all the small factories went down as well. All this area became closed down because of the tunnel. All the jobs round here went down that hole.

This had a profound effect on him and was one of the factors that later led him to stand up to Liverpool City Council in 1978, when they threatened a repeat performance on his next neighbourhood.

In 1966 Tony met and married Joan, who came from the tenements in Burlington Street. After a few house moves in the area, the young couple settled into a tenement flat on Burlington Street in 1973 where they were to remain until they moved to the Eldonian Village in 1989. Tony eventually became the manager of the Jubilee Hall, which was owned by the Church and was the local social club on Burlington Street until the new one was built in the Eldonian Village. He is still, today, the manager of the Eldonians' Social Club.

Throughout all the years he lived in his flat in Burlington Street, Tony was regarded as the person who people went to with any number of problems. This included any repair, maintenance, rehousing and rent disputes. I can recall meetings in his flat in the early 1980s, when there would be a steady stream of knocks at his door. Invariably, it was a neighbour with a 'housing problem' and Tony was expected to sort it out.

George Evans worked for the council's Housing Department in the 1970s with responsibility for these tenements, and he remembers the role that Tony played:

> Tony was like an unpaid councillor; residents would go to him. With the agreement of Paul Orr, the elected councillor, Tony became the first port-of-call for people. I liaised with Tony on management issues, so I'd be quite often talking to him about the problems of someone who needed to be moved on a temporary basis, or someone... whose daughter

> was looking for rehousing and needed to fill in an application form, or general repair problems. Then, if nothing was done about these, Paul Orr would go in and see *my* boss, and he'd take it through that route. We worked as a team.

So at the time of the Archdiocese campaign in 1976, Tony was already known in the community as someone who could sort out problems and get things fixed. The campaign saw him emerge as a leader. When Liverpool City Council announced their plans for demolition of the tenements in Vauxhall in 1978, he knew it was time to take a stand. His main motivation was to prevent his family experiencing the loss of their neighbourhood a second time. He believed that there was 'something better out there than this'. Once it was clear to him that his neighbours also wanted, overwhelmingly, to stay in their neighbourhood he felt obliged to lead them, and then 'there was no way back' from this decision.

His decision to set up in this way was partly based on his solid relationship with Joan, his wife. Tony is clear about her steady and constant support for him:

> We were having the committee meetings in my back room as well. Joan was making sandwiches and all that. She was magnificent in all this, and how she put up with it, I don't know. And we had three kids to bring up. But she knew what we were trying to achieve, and like everyone else, she didn't want her neighbourhood breaking up. So, she believed in what I was doing.

Finally, there is an amusing anecdote that demonstrates his community's faith in him. In 1982 there had been a minor quake in this part of Liverpool, with superficial damage to some buildings. Within a few minutes, an elderly woman knocked on his door to ask, 'What are you going to do about these earthquakes, Tony?' 'I'll look into it, luv,' he replied.

The Tenement Demolition Programme in Liverpool

8

BY 1976 LIVERPOOL CITY COUNCIL had identified 57 slum clearance areas across the city, including most of the 1930s tenements from the south end to the city centre and through to the Vauxhall area in the north. In particular, it meant the demolition of all the tenements around Burlington and Eldon Streets, affecting some 1,500 people.

Like most local authorities in the UK at that time, Liverpool's slum clearance programme was not a comprehensive approach to the regeneration of neighbourhoods. It focused primarily on knocking housing down, clearing sites and rehousing people across the city, wherever it had available properties. It was not possible to move a neighbourhood 'en bloc', as the council had neither the empty stock for this nor the strategy.

Ironically, Liverpool City Council was in a better position than most to have created a coordinated demolition and redevelopment plan, because of its enlightened use of housing associations. Liverpool had one of the largest housing association sectors in England. The sector had the leadership and staff skills to deliver large-scale new-build developments, and to work closely with residents. It appears, however, that the council did not recognize this potential. So one of the few alternatives to the council's approach to slum clearance was for local groups to form a housing cooperative; and it was staff from housing associations who provided development support and capacity building to all of these housing cooperatives.

From the mid-1960s when the Labour Party was running the city council, a large number of high-rise tower blocks had been built in the outlying parts of Liverpool. These blocks were then used to house the dispersed families from the slum clearance programmes. Aside from these tower blocks, there was often little there. Initially, few of them even had shopping facilities let alone any of the basic support services such as health, post offices, etc. And, of course, the people who had to live in these places did not know each other, as they were simply allocated the first available flat. For many it felt like they had moved to another town. They could not visit friends in the old community in the town centre because the area was demolished, and their former neighbours were suffering from the same feelings of loneliness and loss in other city outskirts. The tower blocks had large tracts of land between them for which the residents felt no ownership, and which were soon desolate. Any facilities, such as the crude and ugly playgrounds, were 'undefended' and they too became neglected and eventually destroyed by young teenagers.

It is not difficult to understand, therefore, the fear and anger that people felt when they heard that their inner-city community was to be destroyed. Most people living in the tenements would have agreed that the housing stock and the environment were in need of renewal. It was the prospect of moving to other parts of the city and losing their community that caused most distress. Despite these feelings and a strong reluctance to leave, most communities appeared to lack either the determination or local leadership to galvanize them into opposition.

Another complicating factor throughout this new wave of slum clearance in Liverpool in the 1970s was that the council was then under the control of the Liberal Party, either with a small majority or with no overall majority. Liverpool was unique in this, as no other metropolitan city in England had a Liberal council until 1985. Professor Michael Parkinson, in his book, *Liverpool on the Brink*, provides an explanation for this unusual political development:

> ... in 1973, elections were held for the new Liverpool District Council which was to come into office in 1974, and the Liberals scored a shattering victory, taking many former seats from Labour and decimating the Conservatives. With this began the most unusual decade of municipal politics in Liverpool. Between 1973 and 1983 no party had an overall majority, there were constant hung councils, minority and coalition administrations and confusion... The Labour Party in particular was beset with problems. Its greatest millstone was that during the 1960s it had presided over a massive urban renewal and slum clearance programme, which had brutally transformed the city centre and broken

> up natural working class inner city communities, sending thousands of people to the high rise flats on the overspill estates on the perimeter of the city. The dramatic failure of that policy, and the tenants' rejection of it, turned many voters against Labour.[1]

The Liberal council in the 1970s recognized the need for demolition and the need for new housing to replace the stock in the clearance programme, but it was keen to promote alternatives to council new-build. This was due in part to the Liberals' need to appeal to more than just inner-city working-class voters, and in part to their understanding of the unpopularity among council tenants of the new-build programme that they had inherited from the previous Labour administration. The alternatives they promoted included new-build for sale on land owned by the council; funding housing associations to play a lead role in new-build and improving existing stock; and encouraging new-build housing cooperatives.

The need for demolition of the 1930s tenements across the city was also recognized by the people who worked on them, namely, the staff of the council's Housing Department. George Evans, in the Liverpool Housing Department during the 1970s, was directly involved in this programme. His area of operation covered the whole of the north end of the city, including the tenements in Eldon and Burlington Streets:

> The Housing Department staff could see the reasons behind it. I mean, just looking at the building as opposed to looking at individual people – there were no lifts and so mums had to drag kids and prams up three or four flights of stairs. There was no refuse facility; you took your crap outside and you shoved it down the chute – and that's when they built chutes; before that there were none. There was rubbish all over, and you'd quite often see kids playing with rats at the bottom. It couldn't have been the healthiest place for people to live. Not only that, inside the flats it was quite small; it was horrible. So they were no longer acceptable for people going into the 1980s, although people were reluctant to move. I think a lot of the people that I spoke to in the early days didn't think that there was an option available to them.

George and his colleagues were charged with getting the demolition programme up and running – emptying the tenements by rehousing the tenants.

1 Michael Parkinson, *Liverpool on the Brink* (Policy Journals, 1985), 19.

The grim state of the tenements prior to demolition

The Housing Department staff were told that only limited funds could be spent on repairs during this decanting period, and there were to be no improvements to any of the flats. Maintenance was limited to keeping the buildings watertight and dealing with emergencies related to water, electricity and gas. And for most tenants, the only rehousing offers were for homes on the outskirts of the city.

Jim Dunne, the local parish priest at the time, believes there was a wider council 'agenda' behind this pressure to move people away from this part of the city to the outskirts:

> I've wondered about this since, and I think when they [the local councillors] were in the council and planning the strategy for the city as a whole, probably there was a very good case for pulling the tenements down, because there's no question about it, they were awful places to live. And they also knew that places like Kirkby and Norris Green and the new place in Speke [on the outskirts of the city] had redundant properties [because people did not want to live there] and they felt that

> this was one way that they could clear the decks here and fill up those places outside. I think that was a factor in it. What they hadn't done was to take it further and say 'But wait a minute, are we sowing the seeds of trouble here?'

The news reaches Vauxhall: people swing into action

How did people get to hear this momentous news of the destruction of their neighbourhood? Residents today have vivid recollections of that time. Peggy Hackett, still a local resident, recalls receiving a letter telling her about the demolition and rehousing. Tony McGann was given the courtesy of a visit by the ward councillor, Paul Orr, partly, he believes, because Paul was aware of the way this same issue had been handled with Tony's first family home, and the bitterness this had caused. For John Livingston, another resident at the time, it was a conversation he overheard in the pub – neighbours saying to each other, 'I see they're going to pull these down, what's going to happen to us?' Lillian Grimes also recalls hearing the news on the local grapevine.

Reactions were a mixture of horror and fear, and in some cases, hope for a better home: 'Oh my God, where are we going to live', Rita Potter remembers thinking, 'I was panic stricken, and did not want to move.' Peggy was more pragmatic: 'I think at the time we thought we'd get a house with a garden, as we were very overcrowded. But we didn't want to go anywhere strange, because we were born and bred here.'

But for Tony it was a case of 'here we go again':

> It was a shock. I was born here, I love the people here and I didn't want to live anywhere else. And it wasn't just me saying this, it was hundreds of others as well. People were married into families, they were brought up together, and there was well-developed care for people round here and looking after their neighbours. It was unique.

The full implications for the community were too much to take in at first. For example, Jim Dunne remembers meeting with Tony shortly after it was clear what the council was proposing:

> We had a governors' meeting about the primary school and Tony was on the governing body. He'd come to see me about something and as

> he was going out of the presbytery, he said 'What's on the agenda for this afternoon?' and I said 'I can't recall, but I think we'd better put the tenements on'. He said 'Why, what's that got to do with the school?' I said 'Well if they pull the tenements down, there's gonna be no *kids*'. And he said 'God, of course, no school' and then all his fears about the parish going came to the surface.

The public meeting

These people were not alone in facing demolition. For example, over 500 families living in the tenements at Ashfield and Hopwood Gardens, less than a quarter of a mile away but in a different parish, had decided, whatever their fears, to accept the council's offer of rehousing, and most had left the area. Paul Orr, the local ward councillor, realized, however, that the level of discontent among the residents of the blocks around Eldon and Burlington Streets needed to be addressed. He suggested that Tony should organize a public meeting for all the people who lived there.

Over 250 people attended the meeting. The three local councillors sat alone on the stage looking down on the people below them. Jim Dunne, who was standing at the rear of the hall, detected a state of gloom descending on the meeting:

> ... as the meeting went on you could almost feel paralysis setting in, because the councillors assumed right from the start that the people had accepted the decision. They just simply started to talk about removal allowances and so on.

He realized that, for the councillors, the purpose of this meeting was to reassure the people that the council had their best interests in mind:

> I can't remember the various arguments that they used, but they probably said things like 'Well we're in favour of this because it will give us a better city, people deserve better conditions than this, we're not able to maintain these houses' and so on... And I became more and more frustrated at this, and I thought this is going exactly the way I thought it was going to go. So I thought we've just got to step out of role here and break in. So I did. I stood forward and put my hand up to speak, and I

> was quite conscious that people around were going 'Shh, the priest'! So then I mustered a good loud voice and I said 'Who gave you authority to say that these tenements should come down anyway, in the first place?' and before they could answer there was an outburst of 'Right!' I can remember how that question unlocked an hour and a half of abuse that people threw at these councillors.

People remembered why they did not want to go, and they came back at the councillors: 'You said we would be moved locally, what do you mean by local?' The councillors replied, 'Well it's only just down the road' – meaning the outskirts of the city. The reply came back, 'That's not local' – by 'local' the residents meant 'in the next street'. And finally, as Tony remembers, Councillor Paul Orr said 'Okay, you go and do a survey and present it to the council. Let's see what people's views are.' This was a watershed for Tony: 'I said to the meeting "Well that's the first time we've ever been asked what we want". So we got a survey done and that's how we knew that some 90 per cent of the people said, "Yes, we want to stay in the area".'

The survey

At this point in their history, the people accepted that the tenements needed to be demolished, but they also wanted to stay in the area. None of them had any idea how they could keep everyone together in the area, but their first task was to establish the extent of commitment to finding a way.

The priests offered to help with drawing up the survey, and turned their lounge and dining room into a meeting room for the organizers. Each block of flats was asked to provide two people who would go from door-to-door asking who wanted to stay in the neighbourhood.

'We'd come home from work of a night', recalls Rita Potter, 'we had these big pads, and we would go to everyone's door and explain what's happening. "Do you want to stay in the area, or do you want to move out?" I'd say nine out of ten said they wanted to stay in the area.' However, she was always being asked: 'If we stay, *where* do we go? Because there's no houses to go to and there's no land to build them on.'

Finally, the survey was completed and a colour-coded chart of the results was produced. Jim remembers:

> So, at the end of the day this became a big wall chart with colours and everything like that, so much so that the Housing Department sent a guy up and took a picture of it, it was so helpful! But at the end of the day we knew a hell of a lot about what the actual people wanted.

During this exercise, Tony McGann's position as leader was further consolidated – residents in all the tenement blocks looked to him for leadership, and believed in him. Peggy Hackett recalls:

> And Tony said, 'This shouldn't happen. Everyone should stand up.' Yeah, but how do you do that? We had no nous about standing up to anybody, [but] Tony had sense, because he was a Shop Steward in the Union and that.

When asked why other local communities didn't fight to stay local, Rita Potter said 'because they had no-one behind them, to fight for them, like we did. If we hadn't had Tony McGann, not in a million years would we ever have thought of that.' Jim Dunne explained: 'These people went round doing the survey at Tony's behest. That shows the kind of trust they had in him, and that was something he was able to activate.' While Tony had no plans to lead this campaign, his neighbours, the councillors and the priests were encouraging him to step forward. 'I knew someone had to do it and obviously that someone was me,' he says.

The Eldonian Community Association

There was now a mandate for action. Following the positive result from their survey, they decided that a more formal organization was required to take forward the ambitions and hopes of those who wished to stay. The group decided to name themselves after Eldon Street, as it was in the heart of the community; so in the early 1980s the Eldonian Community Association was formed. Tony McGann was elected by the members of the association as its Chair.

There was now a structure that allowed people to participate in, and to receive feedback on the progress of, negotiations with the city council. Trying to negotiate with Liverpool City Council at that time was no easy task, partly because it was politically in a constant state of flux, with no overall majority and no one to chair the committees. Despite this situation within the local authority, Tony led negotiations with the Liberal councillors at the city level, and with the Housing Department officers at the local level. In this he was supported by Councillor Paul Orr, who was now convinced that local people would not agree to be moved out of the area, and that new plans were required. Tony depended on Paul Orr to 'open doors' within the city and county councils. He has never forgotten how much Paul Orr meant to him, particularly in this early formative stage, and the contribution he made to the community.

Given their forceful personalities and the resounding outcome of the survey, the Eldonians were able to exploit the state of indecision and lack of clear direction within the council. They were determined to come up with options for local people to be rehoused where they wished, rather than where the council had available properties. They seized the initiative and did not give it up until they had succeeded in working up these options with the council.

As one of the council officers charged with emptying the tenements,

The newly formed Eldonian Community Association in 1982. From left to right, Councillor Paul Orr, Jackie Jennings, Harry Burroughs, Mick Dragonette, Sonny Newcombe, John Forrest, Pat Divine, Billy Little, Vera Kavanagh, Tony McGann

George Evans recalls hearing about the Eldonians' organized resistance from Councillor Orr. The officers' experience so far had been that although many people were unhappy about having to move, in the end they all did. Their position in relation to the Eldonians was that, unless told formally by the council, they would continue to make rehousing offers to them.

As part of their negotiations for new options for local rehousing, the Eldonian Community Association dealt with the Liberal Chair of Housing, Chris Davies (who is, in 2007, the Liberal Democrat MEP for the North West of England). He was willing to encourage the Eldonians while staying within the Liberal council's 'housing strategy'. The Eldonians were keen to explore all ideas for how best to meet their objectives, and Davies was willing to listen as long it did not involve a large municipal new-build programme that would be owned and managed by the local authority. It was Chris Davies who suggested to Tony and Paul Orr that the Eldonians should explore the idea of forming a housing cooperative to build new houses in the area.

Eventually, a plan was presented to the members of the Community Association for their consideration. It involved focusing first on the Portland Gardens tenements. As Tony explained,

> Following the survey, we said we would start with the Portland Gardens tenements, mainly because they were in a worse state than the other blocks as they were a bit older, having been built in 1939. We saw this as the first stage in regenerating our area and we would try to accommodate everyone. We also knew that we would have to take the lead ourselves.

This open and fair approach to do what is best for the greater good, combined with their sheer determination, has been a key feature of these people from the outset. Tony and his family lived in the tenements across the street from Portland Gardens, as did Margaret Dragonette and her family. She explained:

> When the survey came back, the Committee saw that Portland Gardens was in a worse state than Eldon Street/Burlington Street tenements, so they decided that they would deal with Portland Gardens first. We were quite happy for that to be done, even though we were from Burlington Street, because we *knew* that no matter how long we had to wait... we were going to get something out of this. So we were quite happy for Portland Gardens to go ahead first.

Both the Eldonians and the city council agreed that the Portland Gardens blocks would need to be tackled in phases and would require a carefully coordinated programme of local decanting. A second survey identified those families in Portland Gardens who wished to be rehoused out of the area by the local authority; those who wanted to stay within the area but remain as tenants of the council; and those who were willing to consider a new idea that would provide new local housing, but under the joint ownership and management of the people who lived in them – a housing cooperative. One hundred and twelve families voted for this final option, even though it was not clear to them what it was and how it would operate. This was the only clearance area of the 57 in Liverpool at that time to commit to creating a comprehensive redevelopment strategy based on local consultation.

For the people wishing to remain within the area and with the council, it was agreed that the Portland Gardens tenements would be re-shaped to take them from four storeys down to two, creating, in effect, two-storey terraced houses. One block would be redesigned as sheltered accommodation for the elderly. The council would lead on this development. At the same time, the 112 Portland Gardens families who had opted for the housing cooperative needed to be rehoused locally temporarily to allow the demolition of their tenements.

The decanting programme was coordinated by the local Housing Department office, led by George Evans, and by Tony McGann. 'There was a great deal of management that needed to be done between Tony and me', George explained:

> to save properties where people had moved out, and to relocate them very quickly to people who needed be rehoused temporarily. When someone from Burlington Street tenements had accepted an offer to move to another part of the city, and they moved house on the Friday, Tony and I would know someone who was in Portland Gardens who would move over there temporarily, so that we could free up the Portland Gardens property and enable them to be demolished or refurbished more quickly.

This work went on for some eighteen months, until all 112 families were temporarily rehoused in other local tenements. The commitment and organization from local people impressed George:

> I think it was at that stage that I saw the worth of tenant involvement – and I mean tenant involvement, not just consultation or even participation – how they *could* make a difference in their own lives, how they could act quickly, quicker than we could, certainly.

He was also very impressed with the way that Tony worked within the restrictions of the local authority while at the same time getting local results:

> It was a great success and I enjoyed working with Tony; he really was very easy to work with. He understood the restrictions that we were under as officers. He understood that he could do things that we couldn't. We might get people who were there hanging back for more home-loss payments and he would go and shake them up; go and have a word with them. By the Monday morning they would have a change of heart.

The Portland Gardens Housing Cooperative

9

THE ELDONIANS NOW knew that they needed 112 houses, that the city council supported their desire to take control, and that a housing cooperative had been suggested as a way forward. Although they were unaware of it at the time, they were following a sound tradition in Liverpool. During the 1970s and 1980s, Liverpool was one of the leading cities in the country for housing co-ops, both rehabilitation and new-build.[1] Two housing associations in the city provided staff and funding to foster and support co-ops throughout Liverpool – Merseyside Improved Housing (MIH), now called Riverside Housing, and Cooperative Development Services (CDS).

In 1982 Chris Davies suggested to the Eldonian Community Association that they contact MIH for some advice. Tony recalls him saying 'these people will work with you, and help you develop a vision of what you are looking for, including a housing cooperative'. Tony continues:

> And that's when you came along Jack and thank God you did! You played a major part in this... When you came along, we started to look at a vision for the neighbourhood. You were one of those super people that worked for MIH. I learned an awful lot from Father Jim Dunne and Paul Orr, but I learned a lot more from you. That's a fact; I learnt

1 The first new-build co-op in the city was at Weller Streets in the south end of the city. They 'broke the mould' in that their scheme was the first of its kind to be taken through the bureaucracy of the Housing Corporation (the regulator of housing associations) and the Department of the Environment. It was a rough ride for those involved, but they got there in the end. Their initial meeting to discuss the idea of a housing co-op was in June 1977 and the last tenant moved in in October 1982.

> an awful lot from you. That's when it started to get interesting because at last we were being shown a way forward by yourself.

I was to be the first 'external' professional to work with the Eldonians. I was employed by MIH and was given an open brief by its Chief Executive, Barry Natton, to explore ways of helping this emerging group of residents. Natton seemed to realize their potential and was supportive of this work even though MIH was not receiving any financial return for its efforts.

I aligned myself very closely with the Eldonians, particularly Tony McGann. I felt that here was a group of people who simply wanted to stay together and to live in decent homes in a safe neighbourhood, and there had to be a way of achieving this basic objective. I decided to base myself in the community and opened an office in one of the empty flats in Portland Gardens. This was intended to be a positive statement to local people that MIH and I were committed to their decision to come up with plans to rebuild their neighbourhood.

Initially, I convinced Tony and those close to him that their goal was achievable as long as people believed in it. We did not become bogged down in the detail of how this long-term strategy would be developed and delivered but focused on the immediate challenges. By the time that other professionals arrived, such as the architects, there was a belief in the community generally that their goal was a worthy one and that, with the right support and advice, it could be achieved. This was the essence of my contribution to the Eldonians and Tony.

Tony is very complimentary about the role I played and he explains why he thinks it was effective:

> The people absolutely loved you Jack, everybody did, because we trusted you… you weren't Jack McBane the professional, you were Jack McBane one of us. You were one of the family, and that's how they looked at you… The thing I remember when we got it all going, we had one of the old tenement blocks and you fitted out a flat with all kinds of things at the expense of MIH! …We had a feeling that we had a guy who's going to stand shoulder to shoulder, even though it's his job to advise us… We had a guy here that was something special.

I remember my first phone call from Tony McGann, saying that he and his committee wanted to hear about housing cooperatives. The call came at a good time for me as I had recently finished work on two new-build co-ops in Anfield and Everton and did not know what I would do next. Soon after the call, I attended a meeting of the Community Association, with some 25 people.

Using slides of existing housing cooperatives, and plans from the ones that I had established, I explained about a co-op, including the advantages and the amount of work involved. While people appeared to be excited to learn that other groups had new homes, and to see the pictures, they did not seem to grasp the concept of a co-op and how it could lead to a new community for them. For Rita Potter, and many of her neighbours, it was not clear. She recalls:

> I couldn't grasp about a co-op; what was it all about and everything. And I came out of that meeting... I said to Tony... 'What's he on about, co-ops?'... I thought it was a brilliant idea but something that'd never happen, you know. The first thing I said: 'What's he know about it, he's from Australia!' Never in a million years did we ever think anything would come off like that.

Billy Little junior didn't believe it either: 'I said "this isn't going to happen". When me mam and dad started going to the meetings and that, I was still sceptical, I thought it was pie in the sky.'

In due course I was summoned to meet with Tony and Paul Orr, the first of many meetings in his flat or 'house' as he called it. Tony informed me that the committee wanted to take this idea further, but was not clear how 112 families could be housed on the four local sites they had identified, which had room for only 51 new houses. Looking back, this was a brave decision by the Eldonians, particularly for the people who had opted to form the housing co-op. They knew it meant they would be taken off the council's rehousing list and would lose the opportunity of a new place to live, without having the guarantee that the housing cooperative idea would ever get off the ground.

Tony, however, recalls that this 'was probably the most exciting period of my life, because I knew it was going to happen'. Despite all the uncertainty about securing the funding for the new co-op houses and the many battles that lay ahead of them, he said, 'What did it for me was the joy of seeing people sitting down and designing their own houses, getting some control of their own lives and developing a sense of ownership of their neighbourhood'. He explained that he had never had that sense of ownership of where he lived, and neither had his neighbours. He had his detractors who regularly accused him of 'leading people down the garden path and taking risks with other people's lives', but they were to be proved wrong in the end.

Let's take over the neighbourhood!

By early 1982 there was an agreement with the Chair of the council's Housing Committee to explore options for new houses for those families interested in the housing co-op, including approval in principle to fund this from the council's own resources. The Community Association committee had already identified four small sites in and around Burlington Street, in the heart of their parish, providing land for 51 new houses. This was as far as the group was willing to go. I told them that for all the work and time it was going to take to do this development, we ought to 'widen our horizons'. It was also at this time that I explained to Tony and Paul Orr that we should 'take over the whole neighbourhood, given that no one seems to be bothered about the state of this area'. They agreed.

On this basis, I identified a fifth site that would accommodate 60 houses. This was the former site of the Ashfield and Hopwood Gardens tenements, also in the process of demolition. Tony was sceptical: 'no one from around here will live up there, because it is in a different parish'. However, with no other options, the Association agreed to include it.

Up to this time most housing co-ops in Liverpool limited themselves to approximately 40 houses. It was not clear why 40 became the norm; perhaps the development advisors – the housing associations – had decided that this was a 'manageable' number for a new group. As with most things they did, the Eldonians decided the size of the co-op would be determined by local need and the demand from residents. In hindsight, their large size gave them 'strength in numbers' and encouraged their strong sense of identity.

In 1982 the Portland Gardens Housing Cooperative was formed. The members elected Billy Little as their chairman. Billy has since died, but his son, Billy junior, still lives in Portland Gardens. Tony has very fond memories of him: 'one of the most wonderful men I've ever met. Billy played a big part in all of this. He was a very, very astute man.'

The new co-op also decided to appoint MIH as its development agent, effectively myself. My brief included bringing in other professionals who would focus on the many issues around the development process for the new houses on the five sites. It also included working closely with the commit-

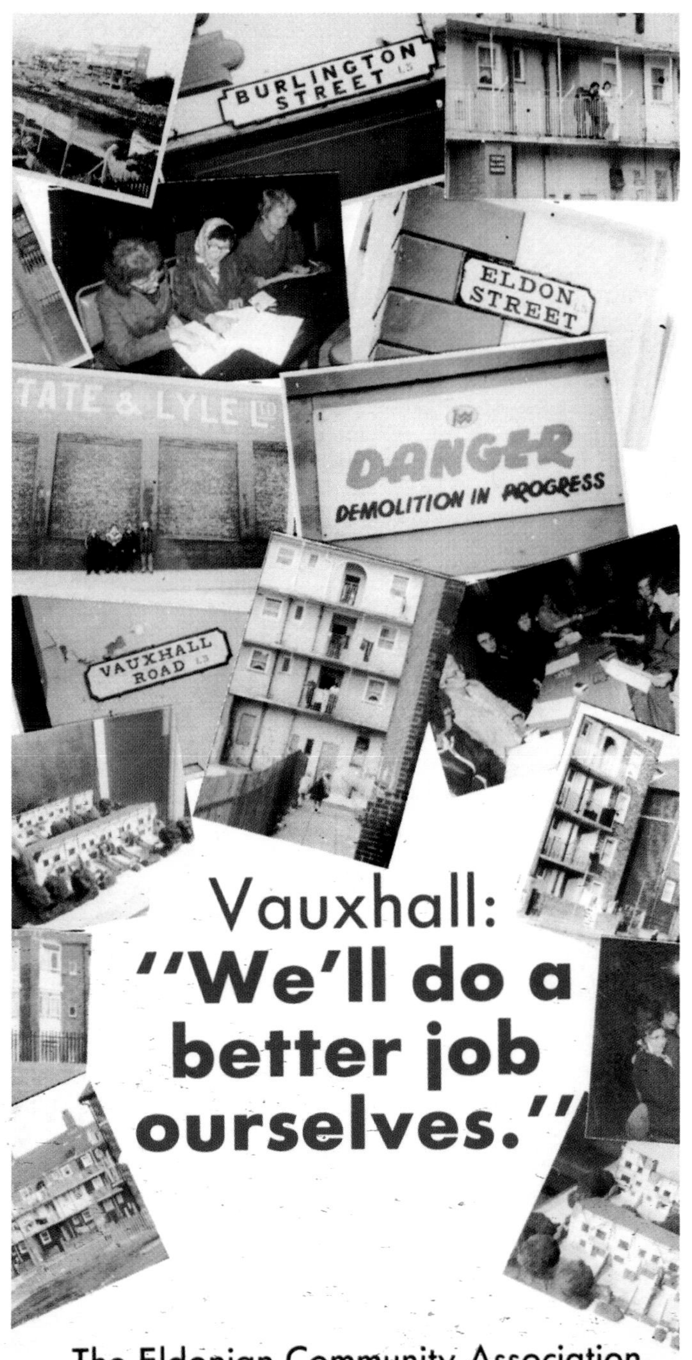

The first leaflet I developed with the Eldonians clearly demonstrates their early mind-set.

The visit of Archbishop Derek Worlock to the first exhibition

Jack McBane and Tony McGann explaining the plans to Jeff (now Lord) Rooker

tees of the Portland Gardens co-op and the wider Community Association, particularly Tony, to instil confidence in the members and to raise the profile of the Eldonians.

I prepared the first Eldonian brochure, which explained the many local problems that we were going to tackle. I also organized their first exhibition. The brochure was entitled *We'll Do A Better Job Ourselves*, reflecting their aspirations and growing confidence that things might get better and that local people were going to have to take the lead on this. As more help arrived from other agencies, including the local authority, the motto became *Better Together!*

The exhibition was mounted in the Jubilee Hall, their social club. It consisted of old photos of the streets and houses, early plans for the sites for the Portland Gardens co-op, and ideas for future projects. It attracted a large number of visitors including Archbishop Worlock and Jeff Rooker, then Labour's spokesman on housing. It proved to be a great success, particularly in giving local people further encouragement that they were not alone in their fight.

Appointing the architects

Another key decision made by the Portland Gardens co-op around this time was to appoint architects to work with them on the design of the proposed new houses on the five sites. The co-op committee asked me to come up with names of firms of architects with suitable experience and skills to do the job. They would interview each firm, including a site visit to one of their recently completed housing projects. In the event they appointed two firms: Vernon Gracie and Partners for the large site and the Wilkinson, Hindle, Halsall and Lloyd Partnership for the four small sites.

They chose Gracie because he had been the main 'on-site' architect for the Byker Wall in Newcastle,[2] and had developed an approach during that project that included living on the site during development and giving residents a major role in the layout and design of their future estate. He used Laurie Chiarella as his job architect for the Portland Gardens project, who soon developed an excellent rapport with the residents. He eventually went on to work for MIH and was to be a key advisor to the Eldonians on their plans during the late 1980s.

2 The Byker Wall is a council housing estate in the city of Newcastle upon Tyne. It was commissioned by the City Council, which appointed the Swedish based architect Ralph Erskine as chief architect. Erskine appointed Vernon Gracie to be his on-site architect. The estate was built in the 1970's and was one of the first schemes in the UK to locally rehouse people from a slum clearance programme.

From the Wilkinson, Hindle, Halsall and Lloyd Partnership came Bill Halsall. From June 1982, when he prepared a feasibility study to assess the capacity of each site, to the present day Bill has been at the centre of every major Eldonian design idea, and is still called on from time to time. He has been a truly loyal servant to the Eldonians.

Bill was born in Liverpool. His practice is still based in the city, and is now called the Halsall Lloyd Partnership. He was the architect for the Weller Streets housing co-op in Liverpool, and had worked on a number of other new-build co-ops in the city prior to meeting the Eldonians. He recalls the process of being interviewed and appointed by the Portland Gardens co-op:

> It was in the tradition of the co-op movement that had grown up over ten years in Liverpool – it was very much focused on this idea of 'we pick our own architect and we are the client' – which was great as far as I was concerned; that's what I was interested in; that's why I was there.

He was also very clear about what people wanted to achieve and their expectations of him:

> They'd been through a process of threat of clearance and dispersal of the community, and that radicalized the community to stay together and be rehoused locally. And what they wanted us to do was to work with them to tackle infill sites around the neighbourhood, produce designs, and supervise construction of the houses to their requirements as a cooperative.

Today the process of an architect working with residents is often inappropriately labelled 'community architecture', when the contact with and level of control exercised by the community is minimal. Bill's approach was community architecture in the truest sense.

Bill describes this link to 'community' as a philosophical root for him. It had evolved during his time at university during the late 1960s. He recalls: 'a lot of things happened, like Ronan Point[3] collapsing, problems of high rise blocks, and the types of things architects had done to communities. And that was seen by me and others as quite a negative role.'

3 Ronan Point was a new tower block built in London's East End in 1968. Two months after opening, an entire corner, from the eighteenth floor to the ground, crashed down in a domino-style collapse. The subsequent public inquiry concluded that the system-built building was structurally unsound, and that a gas explosion had triggered the collapse.

Bill began to redefine the role of the architect in a similar way to Jim Dunne's redefinition of his role as a priest – engaging with the community and their concerns and priorities. This emerging view coincided with a period in London in 1971 where he worked for one of the major practices at the time. The practice worked all over the country and in many parts of the world. He recalls the 'international style' of this era, when the architectural style was more important than the location or the people or the cultural background. He was 'trying to react against that and to think things through from a different perspective, and to work within a socio-cultural context, rather than come up with grand concepts, big ideas that people then had to fit themselves to'.

In time he made his way back to Liverpool and joined with David Wilkinson and Derek Hindle to form the original practice in 1975. David had previously worked in the St Ann's district of Nottingham as well as the Shelter Neighbourhood Action Project in Liverpool in the 1970s. He and Bill, in particular, were very interested in working at the community level and secured much of their early work from the Liverpool housing associations.

The process

Bill and I, with colleagues from MIH, worked closely together to develop a process that would allow the co-op members to understand fully what a housing co-op was, to learn how to manage it, and to participate in the design of their houses. All of us had previous experience of this process, but not on the scale of Portland Gardens. Bill explains:

> We worked with the group and with MIH to get people's preferences of which site they wanted to go on, and then we designed housing that was tailor-made within reason for that group of people. And it was the kind of process that developed a very strong sense of ownership, which was a large part of the reason for doing it... The way I saw it... was a two-way process – the architects were being educated by the people, and the people were being educated by the architects into a common understanding of what was needed.

The Eldonians enjoy illustrating this two-way process with their story of 'the kitchen'. While Bill was guiding them through the complexities of designing their homes, they became increasingly confused by his interpretation of their choices, particularly the location of their downstairs rooms. Then

Bill Halsall working alongside residents in shaping their new community

An early model developed by residents with Bill. The models helped people to express their ideas.

it dawned on them – he needed educating in their terminology! For people from the tenements, the 'kitchen' was their living room; the 'back kitchen' was where they prepared and cooked food. So when they said they would like the sun in their 'kitchen' in the morning, they did not want it lighting up their cooker! As Rita relates:

> I still remember, I said to Bill 'You've got my house back to front'... I'm saying to Bill 'the kitchen' – I meant the living room but I was calling it the kitchen, so he had the house back to front for me! And I'm saying 'No, that's the kitchen' and he's saying 'No, *that's* the kitchen', and I'm saying 'No, that's the *back*-kitchen'... We had poor Bill up the wall, I'm telling you, he didn't know which way! He didn't know our slang.

One of the small group exercises for residents was to measure one of their tenement flats and to compare its area with a plan overlay of the new house standard. This allowed people to 'spatially' relate to a drawing and then to begin to be able to read drawings. Bill also used cardboard models of typical house types with movable internal walls.

Bill and his colleagues also developed a design participation process that would match the order in which formal planning and legal decisions needed to be made. They worked back from the planning application to ensure that community participation was not squeezed by the formal programme schedule. He summed up this design participation process as one of 'putting the bricks and mortar round the community, rather than forcing the community into the bricks and mortar'. I believe he speaks for all the professionals who worked with and for the Eldonians when he describes his feelings for them:

> This was people's lives, livelihoods and hopes and fears and aspirations, and if there was something that didn't work, then you felt a very personal responsibility to the individual co-op member. So there was a very different kind of professionalism in your relationship with a group of people.

Finally, Bill comments on 'community':

> I don't think communities are a sentimental thing. It's as much as anything about networks and support. It's the same as the professional community; it's a network of people who look after each other's kids... helping each other out – mutual self-help. So the co-op model fitted very closely to that community model.

Work continued over a period of some eighteen months to establish the housing co-op, including negotiations with the city council over funding, land issues and the general development process. By the time of the municipal elections in May 1983, the final designs were well advanced and a new house had been allocated to each family.

The demise of Portland Gardens Housing Cooperative

In May 1983 the Liverpool Labour Party won an overall majority in the council elections. The result took most people in the city by surprise, not least the Labour Party itself, which had assumed that it would take another local election to achieve the majority required to run the city council.

In the period leading up to the election, it had become apparent that the Liverpool Labour Party was committed to a large municipal new-build housing programme and was not very interested in housing co-ops. Those of us working in this field were aware of this and realized that a Labour victory in the municipal elections would bring with it some significant changes. In the event, no one had anticipated the extent of these changes and their timing. Within days of their victory, the new Labour council announced they were not interested in 'tenant participation schemes'. By this they meant housing cooperatives. One of the leading Labour councillors told Bishop David Sheppard at the time about their new approach to public housing. He said:

> I believe in public ownership, control and accountability for housing through the elected council. It is the local authority which must satisfy the needs of the working class. Working class organisation in this city lies in the Labour Party and in the unions, not in housing associations.[4]

The irony of this statement, of course, is that the Eldonians were working class, in the Labour Party, and those who had jobs were probably in a trade union.

With the help and advice of Paul Orr, who had again been returned for the Vauxhall ward, negotiations were started quickly with the new Chair of Housing. It was soon apparent that the council did not feel bound by any of

4 Sheppard and Worlock, *Better Together*, 207.

the commitments to housing co-ops made by the previous Liberal administration, and had no intention of honouring them. This included the commitment to the Portland Gardens Housing Cooperative and their new houses. Although the co-op was registered with the Housing Corporation and was in a position to sign legally binding agreements, the land on which the new houses were to be built had not yet been assigned to the co-op. Furthermore, as the main funder for the houses, the council was free to decide how the houses would be allocated.

Negotiations went on until August of that year when the council finally decided it would take over total control of the ongoing development of the schemes on all five sites. Eventually it agreed that the original allocations to the ex-tenants of Portland Gardens would be honoured, but only after a judicial review that ruled in favour of the former members of the housing co-op.

There were a number of reasons given by the new Labour council for their decision. They said that many housing co-ops across the city were self-selecting in their membership, as opposed to allocating new housing solely on the basis of need. This may have been a fair criticism of some of the groups at that time, but not for the Portland Gardens people, as they were all under a demolition programme and this made them top priority for rehousing.

The new council also made it clear that, as the funds for the new housing in Vauxhall came from their allocation from the government, they were within their rights to control the development process and the management of the new schemes. This was undoubtedly true, but it was nonetheless a great blow to the co-op whose members were looking forward to managing and maintaining their own houses. Their experience of being council tenants was not good, which partly explains the initial motto of the Eldonian Community Association: *We'll Do A Better Job Ourselves*. For most of the former members of the Portland Gardens co-op, their greatest fear was having to return to a system of management and maintenance in which they had little or no confidence.

The new council also criticized the previous Liberal administration for putting most of the local authority's 'new-build' housing allocation into housing cooperatives, so that one had to be in a co-op to get a new house. This again may have validity as a general point. However, it does not explain why the people in Vauxhall were not allowed to continue with their scheme, given their status as top priority for slum clearance rehousing.

There were, however, some lighter moments during the tense negotiations between the co-op and the council. Bill Halsall recalls one of these meetings in late 1983 when the councillors insisted that all the new houses were to be fitted with chimneys to accommodate coal fires, partly in support of the then striking miners. At this point, Billy Little, the Chair of the co-op, asked, 'Is this because you all believe in Father Christmas?'

The council finally decided that, in taking over the entire scheme at Portland Gardens, it would not proceed with the designs of one of the architects chosen by the people of Portland Gardens – the Vernon Gracie Partnership. The Gracie designs were innovative. The layout of the houses at the Hopwood and Ashfield site was simple, in consecutive rows to maximize natural light. Exterior stained wood gave them a bright and fresh appearance. And, of course, it was the members of the co-op who were to live in them who had decided on this new and positive look. However, the officers and new councillors did not approve of these designs. They, therefore, appointed the Wilkinson, Hindle, Halsall and Lloyd Partnership to take over this site, and to fit onto it the house types that had been developed for the co-op's small sites. The residents of Hopwood and Ashfield had the comfort of knowing that these more traditional houses had been chosen by their neighbours, but of course they were not the designs that they had developed themselves. Despite considerable anger and disappointment among the former co-op members of the Portland Gardens scheme, and numerous protestations by Tony McGann, Paul Orr and others, the decision was final.

John Livingston was one of many who had worked hard on developing the co-op, as well as on the fight to resist its takeover by the council. He recalls that time with some sadness:

> My own feeling at that time was that we'd lost something really valuable and good, which we'd put a lot of work into. We wanted our estate to be *our* estate; we'd all be like one family, and the houses would be *properly* looked after. Problems would be dealt with by the committee – that's what happens with the Eldonians now – and the higher standards of repairs and maintenance. We knew the council was a very mediocre deliverer of services, and we knew that we'd lost something precious. I think it was a blow to our morale, because we believed the co-op was a good thing and everyone would have respected other people's property and all the rest of it. Our spirits had been crushed by that, and many people who were enthusiastic for the co-op, after a period of time, a couple of years or so, saw the way it [the estate] was going, so they got out, left.

There were a number of immediate consequences of the termination of the co-op project. I no longer had any role to play in the development of the project and concentrated my attention on the next phase of the regeneration, namely the Tate & Lyle site and the early planning of the Eldonian Village. In May 1984 my family and I left Liverpool and moved to Sheffield, although I continued to work with the Eldonians on a part-time basis for a further year.

More significant, however, was the effect this decision was to have on the Eldonians. Throughout the negotiations with the council, the councillors had told Tony McGann that he should take his community's concerns about council decisions through the Labour Party system, starting with their local ward party. Once the battle for Portland Gardens was lost, Tony realized that if their lives could be so affected by political decisions, then as a community they must become part of the political system:

> I reminded people that we had set out to regenerate the area ourselves, and we'd got to do something about it, and the only way to do something about it was to get involved in the politics. And it was the best thing we've ever done. That was the night I rounded up about a hundred odd people, went along to the local Labour Party ward meeting and we took all of them on.

The model developed by the Vernon Gracie Partnership, which was never built.

They all joined the local Labour Party, and from then on attended ward party meetings. Soon it was local people who controlled the ward party, local people were elected to sit on the council, and so the people of Vauxhall's interests were represented in the political arena. While they had confidence in Paul Orr and recognized his commitment to the area, they were determined that only people from their area would become selected to stand for election to the city council. Paul Orr fully backed their position on this.

This action was another milestone in the development of the Eldonians. It was a decision they made entirely on their own, as they did not require any of their professionals to advise them on something as fundamental as this. This decision to take control of their local political machine was as instinctive as their decision to remain in Vauxhall and resist any attempts by the council to winkle them out. It sent out powerful messages across the city, partly because up to then, local community groups did not 'get involved in politics'. They were now stating very publicly that they were not going to be bullied or manipulated by the council, or by anyone else for that matter. They would engage in politics to protect and extend their plans for their new neighbourhood. Perhaps it was also a declaration of their self assurance or 'coming of age'.

Bishop David Sheppard and Archbishop Derek Worlock presenting their book to Tony McGann

The two religious leaders showing their support, this time with Jack McBane and his son Will; Paul Orr looks on from the right

Throughout the period of trying to convince the council to allow the co-op to proceed, the Eldonians received considerable support from around the city, and in particular from their old friends, Archbishop Derek Worlock and Bishop David Sheppard, the Anglican leader. These two men stood together on a wide number of issues for the betterment of Liverpool, despite some public criticism. Both had expressed their public support for what the Eldonians were trying to achieve, mainly on the basis of David Sheppard's long-held view that inner cities could only survive and prosper if the skilled residents remained living there. He recognized in Tony McGann just such a person, and when Tony and I first met him in his office, he committed to help to keep this community together. The title that Derek Worlock and David Sheppard gave to their book in 1988, was, of course, *Better Together*, which was by then the motto of the Eldonians!

Today Tony acknowledges this invaluable support from the two Bishops:

> I think it was very important. A lot of people looked up to the Church and what was significant about this support, I began to realize, was that it was not just about going to church, it was about coming out.

> This is where the likes of Father Dunne and Michael Lane, Archbishop Worlock and Bishop Sheppard were different from any clergy that we'd ever known. So I think that because they gave us their backing, this made it easier for local people to support it as well. Jim Dunne came to the front, Archbishop Worlock, Bishop Sheppard, they all came to the front; they all made it quite clear in the papers 'we're going to stand with you'. Archbishop Worlock actually said 'we'll stand shoulder to shoulder with them'. So that was significant because it gave that extra hope to people.

Finally, the last word on this episode is Tony's: 'It's the easiest thing in the world to break a community up; it's a lot harder to build it up again'.

Conclusion

The last four chapters have covered the years 1976 to 1983 for the Eldonians. During this relatively short period they travelled a long way. Their lives had been turned upside down, from the plans of the Archbishop of Liverpool to reorganize their local parishes, through the decision of Liverpool City Council to knock down their neighbourhood and move all its inhabitants across the city, to the dashing of their hopes for a housing co-op in Portland Gardens. However, despite all this upheaval, the people who lived in the area around Eldon Street in Vauxhall were now in a better position than at the outset of this period of their history.

First, they had firmly and widely decided that they intended to stay in this community, even if it was not yet clear how this was to be achieved. Secondly, they were adamant that they would be in full control of the developments required to achieve their first objective. Thirdly, they had gathered around them a number of strong and well-organized allies, including their local priests, committed professionals and organizations who shared their vision, and key Liverpool leaders, specifically the Archbishop and Bishop. And finally, they had in Tony McGann a brave and energetic leader.

Despite the major setback of having their first redevelopment project taken off them, the Eldonians were more determined than ever to continue with their key objectives. Most other community organizations and neighbourhoods would have thrown in the towel at this stage, and if they had, it would have been understandable. But not these people. There were still some 145 families living in the tenements at Burlington and Eldon Streets, including Tony McGann's own family, and all of them were determined to stay in Vauxhall.

So despite the appearance of having been beaten by Liverpool City Council, this short period of their history had produced the core elements of their ultimate success. There was a strong and well-supported local organization, the Eldonian Community Association, chaired by someone who was not going to be intimidated. The local people were now in control of their local Labour Party, and they had declared publicly that they opposed the style and politics of the people who took over Liverpool City Council in 1983. The Eldonians now knew that they and their professionals would receive no favours from Liverpool City Council. They also realized that they had become the 'David' to the council's 'Goliath', and that this battle would be conducted in public, as the rest of the city looked on from the sidelines.

They and their professional advisors now turned their hand to the new challenge – to create a 'place' in their area, under their control, with homes for the 145 families of Burlington and Eldon Streets. All eyes turned to the site of the abandoned Tate & Lyle sugar refinery that had closed down in 1981. This piece of severely polluted and abandoned land was to become the home of the world-class Eldonian Village.

10 Liverpool in the 1980s

At the end of the previous chapter the first major housing project developed by the Eldonians at the Portland Gardens tenements was taken back under the control of Liverpool City Council, following the council elections in May 1983. In order to understand the subsequent course of events, it is necessary also to understand the state of Liverpool at the time.

Although they had to fight hard for their dream, the Eldonians were also in the right place at the right time. Their desire to remain in their neighbourhood coincided with a series of developments in Liverpool that eventually had a direct effect on their plans for new homes. This chapter, therefore, explains the state of the city during the 1980s, before subsequent chapters resume their story.

Liverpool in the early 1980s

In the early 1980s the city of Liverpool was facing a number of deep-seated problems. Some of these it suffered in common with other British cities, but others were specific to the city and would require local solutions. Economically, the city was in the middle of a general decline that was nationwide, but seemed to hit Liverpool more than many other places:

> Between 1979 and 1981 the rate of job losses accelerated to a frightening level, employment in the city falling by a further 18 per cent. By early 1981, 20 per cent of the city's labour force was unemployed

> and it was reported that there were just 49 jobs on offer for the 13,505 youngsters registered unemployed. De-industrialization was turning Liverpool into a 'graphic illustration of urban dereliction' and it was no coincidence that the 'People's March for Jobs' of May 1981 began in the city. Seemingly everywhere stood empty factories, boarded shop fronts and tracts of wilderness as some 15 per cent of property in Liverpool was either derelict or vacant by the end of the 1970s. From a peak census population of 855,000 in 1931, the numbers living in Liverpool had halved by the 1960s as people streamed out of a city that seemed to be in its death throes. Across the city the talk was of the closure of this or that plant: Dunlop, BICC, Plessey, GEC, Lucas, Girling, Courtaulds, Meccano. Every industry had been hit.[1]

At the neighbourhood level, local entrepreneurs and shopkeepers closed down their businesses as more and more inner-city communities were demolished by the city council through its ongoing programmes of slum clearance.

Socially, there was considerable unrest and a sense of alienation among many people. The city seemed to have lost its way and there was little confidence in things getting better in the near future. Large tracts of land across the city's inner area were empty except for the old streets and the occasional pub, again from the clearance programmes. People had been displaced, usually to the outskirts where they had few contacts, and they were unaccustomed to living so far from the centre of town. Life on most of the 1960s housing estates was grim with poor environments, a lack of decent facilities and decreasing maintenance by the city council. Back near the city centre, the long-established black community that lived mainly in the Granby area of Toxteth in south Liverpool was becoming increasingly angry, feeling that they were suffering the consequences of this decline more than others in the city. They also felt that they were being victimized by the police. Some public officials with whom I worked at that time in Liverpool often described their work as managing the city's decline rather than leading on its regeneration.

Politically, before the local elections in 1983, the city was in a constant state of infighting between the Labour Party and the Liberals. There were continuous hung councils, minority and coalition administrations, and times when the council's committees had no Chair. The electorate appeared to have little respect for either party. According to Parkinson, they held Labour

1 Jon Murden, 'City of Change and Challenge: Liverpool since 1945', in Belchem (ed.), *Liverpool 800*, 428–29.

A scene from the riots, which were to have a significant effect on developments in the city for some years

responsible for the destruction of so many inner-city working-class communities; and few seemed to know what the Liberals stood for.[2] The outcome of this political stalemate was that the city council had little or no credibility and showed few signs of leadership. It was not in a position to lead the city out of its state of decline.

Michael Parkinson puts this lack of leadership from the council into perspective:

> ... the demoralising impact of ten years' paralysis upon the politicians and officers cannot be understated. It was a crucial lost decade for the city. Decline would have been difficult to manage if the city had had enlightened leadership. That it had to endure such political incoherence instead seemed a cruel stroke of fate.[3]

2 Parkinson, *Liverpool on the Brink*, 30.

3 Parkinson, *Liverpool on the Brink*, 24

The Liberal administrations in the 1970s and early 1980s further compounded the problems for the city council. They were keen to keep council spending low in order to appeal to the middle classes, with unfortunate consequences, as Lord (Patrick) Jenkin explains. Jenkin was Secretary of State for the Environment between 1983 and 1987, with responsibility for dealing with Liverpool City Council:

> The financial disciplines that we were trying to impose struck Liverpool harder than most other major cities. The Liberals leading Liverpool had kept council spending down, and because that tended to be the benchmark for future spending, it meant that *their* spending had to be kept very tightly under control under the rules; and Liverpool was hit very hard by that.

In July 1981 rioting broke out in the Granby area of Toxteth. This was the first serious urban riot in a British city in modern times. It lasted for nine days and resulted in the destruction of some 71 buildings, 500 arrests and some 450 police officers injured. At one level it was triggered by the arrest of a local young black man but it soon took on a much wider significance for the city. I recall that the whole city was in a state of shock, and no one seemed to know what to do about this violent outburst. In some ways the riot brought things to a head, as people soon began to talk to each other and came to some understanding about the scale of the problems facing the poor and unemployed people of the city.

Government intervention in Liverpool

In the face of all these troubles, the Conservative government, led by Margaret Thatcher, took dramatic action. They had inherited from the previous Labour government an arrangement whereby government ministers were given responsibility for leading local partnerships in specific cities. In the national election of May 1979 Michael Heseltine (now Lord Heseltine) was appointed Secretary of State for the Environment, with responsibility for Liverpool. He still held this post in 1981. He picks up the story:

> It wasn't until 1981 when the riots took place that I suddenly realized that the situation was a great deal worse than we had been aware, and

> said to the Prime Minister 'Can I take three weeks off to really try to understand exactly what's going on in the urban area'. She agreed, and I spent three weeks in Liverpool full-time, meeting people of every background; and then another eighteen months trying to help sort out some of the problems. It was that last eighteen months, and the intensity of it, that created the image of a Minister for Merseyside.

Heseltine's reasons for committing himself to the problems of Liverpool were, first, that he felt a sense of responsibility for the city that some people had set out to burn, and this reflected on his stewardship. Secondly, he wanted to find out *what* had gone wrong, and he didn't believe he could do that by sending civil servants and receiving a file on the situation. He was also very conscious that having so publicly committed himself to understanding the causes of the problems, he was also raising local expectations that he was going to do something about them.

At the end of his three weeks, having listened to a wide range of people who told him what they thought was wrong, he was most struck by 'the dearth of leadership in the city'. Heseltine concedes that this was against a background of many problems that had been imposed on Liverpool, such as the loss of its manufacturing base and jobs. However, 'that wasn't the whole of it in any way. It was the fact that there was no one really with the wit and the will and the energy to try and pull the thing together and give a powerful lead.' And it was this that he committed to do over a period of eighteen months.

Looking back some twenty-six years later, it can be argued that Michael Heseltine set the foundations for urban regeneration that are still in place today. He used his time on Merseyside to put into practice his basic philosophy for success. In summary, over the eighteen months, he put in place:

- An agenda for action that included some 30 projects that came out of his three weeks of listening. Most of these would eventually receive direct capital funding from the government.
- The Merseyside Development Corporation. The legislation for Urban Development Corporations was established in 1979 and enacted in 1981. These effectively bypassed local authorities and had powers of land acquisition, planning and funds that came direct from government.
- A Merseyside Task Force. He established this in the autumn of 1981, comprising a group of bright civil servants and top young executives, seconded from the private sector and from local organizations. The Task

Michael Heseltine on his highly publicized tour of Merseyside in 1981

Force had direct access to Heseltine and all other government ministers, and had its own budget. Its leader, Eric Sorensen, was an excellent choice, as he seemed to share many of the same values and approach as his boss.

- An instruction to Liverpool City Council that they had to work with the local private sector – by which they thought he meant the Chamber of Commerce – and to do this there needed to be a formal partnership.
- Additional funding to the existing Urban Programme that provided capital funding. This was called the 'Urban Grant', and was mainly a revenue fund that provided the 'money that oiled the wheels of the partnership arrangements'.
- A Derelict Land Grant Programme within the Urban Programme funds. Heseltine quickly realized that much of the land in and around the city centre had a negative value and so would not attract private investment, in particular house builders. To entice them into the city centre, he used this Derelict Land Grant to tackle issues such as contamination and abandoned foundations from previous users, thus removing the land's negative value and restoring it to a state that was ready for development. As he says:

> Basically, what I was saying: 'I have this money. I'll eliminate the negative value. If it's full of toxic waste, I'll take it away, until it's a site that the private sector will use.' Well, that, of course, had the immediate consequential effect of bringing the two sides together, and enhancing public expenditure.'

The last major change in his approach to regeneration was that when an organization came forward with a piece of land that it wanted to develop, it had to demonstrate what it proposed to do on that land, and explain who was going to do it. As Heseltine says, 'this was, as it sounds, so basic, sensible and obvious and easy, [but] it was revolutionary in 1981!'

Lord Heseltine is proud of his many achievements during his eighteen months as 'Minister for Merseyside'. He explained what he saw as his 'philosophy':

Albert Dock, saved from demolition and today a popular landmark in the city (photo © webbaviation.co.uk)

> The biggest outcome was a confidence in the philosophy behind the policy. I believed that leadership was missing, and as a Tory I believe leadership is a vital side of human society. As a moderate Conservative I believe in partnership, and communities working to a better attainment than perhaps individuals could achieve. I believe that where there is power and wealth, there is obligation, which is a very paternalist conservatism – *noblesse oblige*, call it what you like, I don't mind as long as you get on with it. And also that deep down I was applying competitive principles. What I was actually doing was removing negative value in order to enable deprived areas, once they'd lost the negative value, to compete.

Heseltine had changed the rules of engagement and suddenly things began to happen, including developments that seemed impossible only a year before. Many of these developments are still successful today. They include the restoration of the historic Albert Dock; the mixed housing development in the precinct of the Anglican Cathedral; and the Wavertree Technology Park that helped to create over 1,000 jobs.

At Knowsley, a very traditional Labour authority, Heseltine helped create a new model for the reordering of failed housing estates. Cantril Farm (known locally as Cannibal Farm) was just another overspill estate for people from the city centre, with all the signs of decline and hopelessness. He persuaded the Labour leader, Jim Lloyd, the Housing Corporation, a bank and house builders to come up with a new, mixed community with its own legal structure. The estate was refurbished, and new community facilities were built, as well as new houses for sale. It was renamed Stockbridge Village and was owned by its own housing trust. Tom Baron, a private house builder and advisor to Heseltine, chaired the new trust initially. The experiment worked, and the former drab and failing housing estate soon began to improve. This approach and formula is still used today by government and housing authorities to turn around failing housing estates.

The effect on the Eldonians of all this intervention was to be significant. Although Michael Heseltine did not work directly with them – as he was moved to Defence in January 1983 – his new local structures and a new method of funding that came direct from government was to be the answer to their prayers for the Tate & Lyle site.

Local government in Liverpool in the mid-1980s

In May 1983 there were national and local government elections. Nationally, the Conservatives were returned to power and a new Secretary of State for the Environment was appointed, Patrick Jenkin. In Liverpool, the Labour Party won a clear majority in the local council elections, its first since the early 1970s. The new council was much more militant in its approach to solving the problems of the city and was not interested in reaching a compromise with the new Tory government on its budgets or its approach to housing. Patrick Jenkin inherited a situation that he describes as one that 'none of my predecessors had to face'.

Michael Parkinson gives an explanation of the origins of the new type of Labour Party councillor who won control of the council:

> From the late 1970s a new breed of activist began to join the Liverpool Labour party, filling the vacuum left by a generation of inadequate representatives. They were younger, more willing to work hard, more committed, more ideological, and often, though not always, members of the Militant Tendency.[4]

The new council inherited a comparatively low level of government funding from the previous Liberal administration, and by 1983 cuts in government allocations to local authorities were beginning to bite. Parkinson explains that for Liverpool City Council to sustain levels of service delivery from the previous year (i.e. the last Liberal administration) would have required a rate rise of some 42 per cent and Margaret Thatcher's government was not going to allow that to happen:

> In fact, after Labour won the council election in May [1983] it ran the city on the Liberal budget for 1983/84. But spending ran far beyond £212M (the budget) and caused a large deficit at the end of the financial year. And that was the point of departure for Labour's confrontation with the [Conservative] Government in 1984 and afterwards.[5]

4 Parkinson, *Liverpool on the Brink*, 25.

5 Parkinson, *Liverpool on the Brink*, 32.

The story of the standoff between the Conservative government and Liverpool City Council between 1983 and 1987 has been the subject of a number of books, including Parkinson's. It is important only as a background issue for the Eldonians' story, as it impacted on some of the developments in Vauxhall, about which we will hear later.

11 Phase 1 of the Eldonian Village: Securing the Land and Funds

Now we return to the Eldonian story. This phase of their journey is complex, spanning 1982 to 1989, with different strands running in parallel. It features the Eldonians in the figure of their leader, Tony McGann, and his trusted professional advisors. Their story is a testament to his ability to win the trust and loyalty not only of his friends and neighbours, but also of professionals and politicians alike. It is also a testament to his commitment to his local community, his tirelessness, his sheer stubbornness and his willingness to trust and learn from others. And finally, it is a testament to the integrity and commitment of the professionals and their agencies whose hearts he won.

As we have seen, at the time that they were planning and fighting for Portland Gardens, the Eldonians were also looking for other sites to allow the remaining 145 families to stay in the area. These included Tony McGann and his family, living in the old tenements at Burlington and Eldon Streets.

In 1981 an event occurred that was totally outside their control – the closure of the Tate & Lyle sugar refinery in Vauxhall. With hindsight, the Eldonians were to see this as a blessing as well as a curse; at the time, however, it was purely a curse. Around 1,700 jobs were lost, most of which were local. As many families had more than one member working there, the closure put whole families out of work in one go, and for many it was to be their last job. The blessing, which only emerged as time passed, was that the 22-acre site offered the chance to rehouse the remaining 145 families.

The Tate & Lyle factory; the tenements at Portland Gardens and Burlington Street can be seen top right (photo © Mills Media)

The Tate & Lyle site

This site was one of the 30 projects on Heseltine's 'agenda' described in the previous chapter. When the company abandoned the site, it was transferred to the ownership of English Estates, a government agency concerned with the development of business parks and industrial estates. Following discussions between the Merseyside Task Force and English Estates, it was decided that the first challenge was to demolish the buildings, and following this the condition of the land would be investigated. Michael Heseltine personally called the Chairman of Tate & Lyle and extracted some £400,000 for the cost of the demolition.

The demolition and site clearance went on for most of 1982 and into 1983. It was not obvious to either the Merseyside Task Force or English Estates what could be done with this large area of former industrial land which was likely to be severely contaminated. Given the trend of industry leaving Liverpool over the previous few years, it was not likely to attract any private company looking to relocate, and it certainly was not going to be attractive to any private house builder as the surrounding area was almost totally composed of poor council housing.

The Eldonians and their advisors, however, knew what *they* wanted to do with it, and wasted no time in introducing themselves to the local manager of English Estates, Bill Locke. We met him frequently during this period, and although community regeneration was not part of his brief, the Eldonians worked their charm on him and he soon understood where they were coming from and came to admire their determination and courage.

In the event, the Merseyside Task Force and English Estates decided to hold an ideas competition. The introduction of competitions into regeneration was another of the new approaches introduced by Heseltine, and he would use it again a few years later when he launched the City Challenge initiative. Up to this point, most new developments were either private-sector investments or local authority schemes, usually new housing estates. Heseltine was keen to break this traditional approach and the Tate & Lyle site was to become a good example of the principles he brought to Merseyside during his eighteen months there.

The ideas competition

The ideas competition for the Tate & Lyle site was announced in 1982. It was co-ordinated by English Estates and was open to whoever wished to enter. As the title makes clear, the sponsoring organizations were seeking ideas for potential uses for the land. They were not seeking fancy designs or details of funding packages or a master plan for the area. They wanted ideas and the Eldonians and their friends had plenty of those.

The Eldonians, MIH and Bill Halsall started to pull together ideas that had been discussed in the past, new ones from other projects, including projects in the USA, and ones that suited the conditions in which they were now living. There was also the experience from Portland Gardens and the work with the architects that was getting under way, including ideas that co-op members had picked up from the many visits to successful housing projects elsewhere as part of their learning about design and house layout.

6. NEIGHBOURHOOD
DEVELOPMENT CORPORATION

- under local control
- to own land
- to sub-divide – leases
- with a caretaker role
- to sponsor workers co-ops and small businesses
- to channel finance
- to liase with national and local government agencies
- with a 'resource' function – giving business advice and services reskilling the community – running training schemes

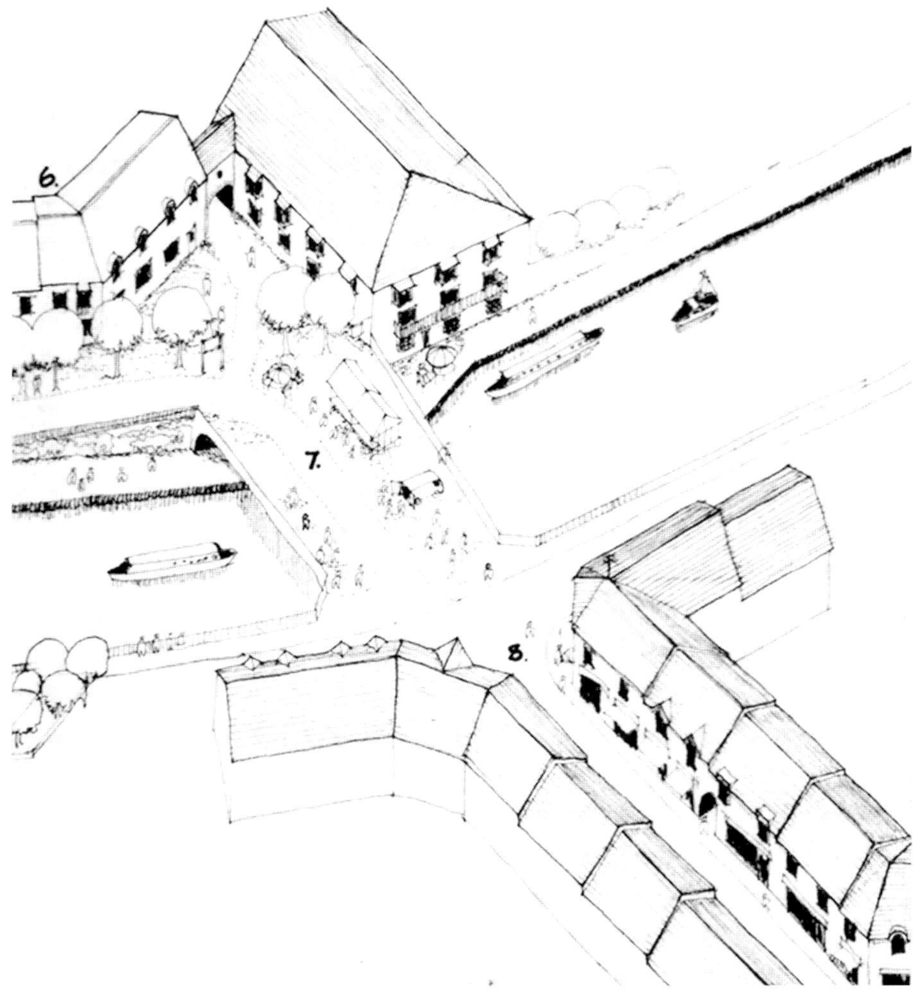

A page from the 1982 Self-Regenerating Community bid

While none of us at that time had any direct experience of economic development or job creation projects, it was clear that an approach was required that addressed a number of key local issues. These included new housing, training opportunities, shops, new enterprise, leisure facilities, all to be owned and managed by a local development trust. The plan was centred around the Leeds/Liverpool canal which was in a terrible state of dereliction, but which would eventually be regenerated and form the focus of the 'village'.

The bid was put together by Bill Halsall, and Tom Clay from MIH. It was called 'A Self-Regenerating Community', and it was a bid by local people to take over their neighbourhood, offering a range of necessary services and facilities, all to be locally controlled. A separate bid was also submitted by the City Architect of Liverpool City Council. It included a similar range of housing and new facilities but did not include any local involvement in the planning or eventual management. All those involved in the Eldonian bid had high hopes and believed that these were the type of ideas that English Estates was looking for. But again, disaster was just around the corner.

One of the rules of the competition was that the entrants were not to discuss their bid with the local press. In his enthusiasm about our bid, Tony McGann mentioned it to a journalist for the *Catholic Herald*, a paper with a very small circulation. Somehow this leaked out to the main Liverpool press, and English Estates had no choice but to disqualify us. There had been many highs and lows up to this point, but this was a big disappointment to everyone involved. There was nothing to be done about it. The city council's bid won by default and they were awarded the prize of £6,000.

We consoled ourselves with the belief that although we had been disqualified, ours was a more imaginative bid that had originated in, and was owned by, the community. We also convinced ourselves that English Estates thought the same way, although we had no real idea about this. More than anything else, we felt very sorry for Tony, as he felt personally responsible for the disqualification. We also believed that with it went any chance of obtaining possession of the site.

However, it was not in the nature of the Eldonians or their advisors to give up. A chink of light appeared and we went for it. Another rule of the competition was that English Estates was not bound to *implement* the winning bid. We waited some time for the dust to settle and then went off to meet Bill Locke again at English Estates. He sympathized with us and indicated that his organization had been impressed with our bid and wanted to explore it further with us. This was now our opportunity to present the ideas behind the submission, and to convince key decision-makers of its feasibility and the extent of local commitment. We were back in the game!

We realized that we were in new territory in the sense that we wanted to create a neighbourhood like no other in the UK at that time. It would be a place large enough to house the remaining families in the area, and would offer others the opportunity to return to Vauxhall. It would have all the facilities and services a neighbourhood requires, and it would be owned and managed by people who lived in it. Its development would be based on regular consultation and participation. No one could come up with any sound reasons why such a development could not work and we had an ally in English Estates that was willing to allow us to develop our thinking. This was the beginning of the 'Eldonian Village'.

Making friends and influencing people

With new hope, the Eldonians and their advisors ran a campaign from 1983 to 1987. The two goals were to secure the land at Tate & Lyle, and to secure the funds for its reclamation and the building of 145 houses. It was now mid-1983 and the new Labour-controlled council, which had recently taken back full control of the housing co-op at Portland Gardens, had said that it did not 'believe in any tenant participation schemes'. So we knew that we would receive no support from that quarter. However, Michael Heseltine had already included the reclamation of the Tate & Lyle site in his 30 projects. He had also introduced into the city a potential route for securing approvals and funding for *development* on the site that would not require the approval of the city council. In order to take advantage of this, we had to get our building project included in a list of housing schemes being drawn up by the Secretary of State/Merseyside Task Force, which would receive direct government funding. This funding was a Special Allocation for Merseyside, introduced in 1982, and administered by the Task Force and the Merseyside Office of the Housing Corporation. So, while we realized we had a big challenge to present our case and to convince people to fund it, we also knew that there now existed on Merseyside the framework and the potential funding for such projects, thanks to Heseltine's intervention.

First we began to meet with key people in Liverpool who we believed would

The 'new' co-op office on Eldon Street; the Portland Gardens sign was kept for old times sake

be interested in the ideas and would have influence. The initial aim was to present the plan for moving 145 families from the tenements to new homes on the Tate & Lyle site and, hopefully, to secure their support in principle. These people included Archbishop Worlock, who quickly and publicly committed himself; Bishop David Sheppard, who was also supportive as he recognized the need to keep this community together, and in Tony McGann the leadership skills to do it; Mike Clarke and Max Steinberg at the Housing Corporation, who told us that while they did not have the funds as yet, they supported the ideas; and Barry Natton, the Chief Executive of Merseyside Improved Houses, my boss, who agreed to continue funding my post.

Everyone was encouraged by the positive reactions from these key people. They provided an endorsement that was critical at a time when we were not yet convinced that we could ever secure the considerable amount of public funds needed for the project.

'Covering all the bases': Tony leaves his 'house' with David Steel, the Liberal Democrat Party Leader on a tour of the area. Tony's wife Joan (on the left), and daughter Lisa, can be seen in the background.

A second strand of the campaign to win over hearts and minds was a programme of public exhibitions and tours around the area. The Eldonians had a great advantage over many other similar community projects that were also chasing this 'special' fund. They had their own team of professionals who would be on hand for these exhibitions. We used the submission from the ideas competition and the drawings from the projects at Portland Gardens, and we mounted exhibitions in the Jubilee Hall.

As well as the display, we organized tours around the area to ensure that all the visitors had a good understanding of the conditions in which local people were living. There was a new project office in the Eldon Street tenements and the tour would usually end up there for a cup of tea and an 'extracted' indication of where they stood in terms of their support for the project. There was always an up-to-date brochure on our plans for the future to give them. The Eldonians' motto had changed from *Better Ourselves* to *Better Together*, in the new spirit of partnership which was becoming the buzzword on Merseyside.

Among the people who visited the area during this time were the senior staff of the Merseyside Task Force, the Housing Corporation, Liverpool City

Council, national political figures, particularly those with an interest in funding, housing or regeneration, Merseyside Development Corporation and the local housing associations. While this was not explicit lobbying, it was important to make these people aware of the local conditions, the scale of support from the community and the professional approach of the Eldonians.

Finally, as part of the campaign for funding from the Special Merseyside Allocation, the Eldonians asked the Liverpool Bishops – Archbishop Worlock and Bishop Sheppard – to speak directly to key government people to explain the scheme's merits and the need for direct funding. In *Better Together* the Bishops say that they often put the Eldonian project on their agenda in meetings with the Secretary of State.[1] Certainly the government was aware of their support of the Eldonians. As Lord Jenkin recalls,

> Both of them, in their own way, were acutely aware of the conditions in which Liverpool citizens, mostly, were living. They were both very keen to use such influences they had, to promote the changes that would lead to an improvement.

Goal 1: securing the land

The first stage in the long period of the development of the site was to obtain the first option on the land – a commitment from English Estates that the Eldonians would have the first opportunity to buy it. Once that was obtained, we would have more status in our struggle for the funds.

Our campaign following the ideas competition seemed to have reaped benefits. First, English Estates decided not to proceed with the concept submitted by the city council, and agreed to discuss our plans for the site. Secondly, early in 1984 the Board of English Estates agreed to visit the area and meet with the Eldonian Committee and its advisors. Sir Christopher Wates, of the Wates Construction Group and the Wates Foundation,[2] chaired the Board. There was an instant rapport between Tony McGann and Chris Wates, and the latter seemed to appreciate the importance of the Eldonians' cause.

Wates and his Board inspected the exhibition in the Jubilee Hall and listened carefully to the ideas put forward by the local people, including the 'failed' bid from the ideas competition. It became obvious to us that they

1 Sheppard and Worlock, *Better Together*, 210.

2 The Wates Foundation is a large fund supporting charitable work in the built environment and its impact on society.

Celebrating the land transfer to the Eldonians. From the left: Rob Bennett, English Estates (who replaced Bill Locke), Tony McGann, Archbishop Worlock, Sir Chris Wates

had been well briefed prior to the meeting, and that this visit was more of a confirmation of what they already knew about the Eldonians. After nearly two hours of discussion, Wates told us that he was impressed by what he had heard from his own staff and from the people present in the meeting. In fact, he said he was so impressed that he intended to recommend to the Board at their next meeting that the Eldonians be offered first option on the Tate & Lyle land. This was, of course, greeted with delight and relief. At last, someone important had confirmed that our bold new idea made good sense, and was willing to back us.

McGann was feeling lucky that night. Following this great news, he escorted Wates to his vehicle, and tried his hand a second time. He asked him if he would also support the Eldonians in a bid to the Wates Foundation for a new minibus, to replace the old grey 'battle bus'! To his surprise, Wates agreed, and in time the new bus arrived.

Another hurdle was cleared, but another one lay just around the corner. There was a small strip of land in the middle of the site, which had formerly been the canal. At some point Tate & Lyle had filled in this part of the canal and built on it. During the land search by English Estates, they realized that this strip of land was owned by British Waterways, the national body with responsibility for canals. British Waterways staff, knowing that the site was now in demand, set a very high figure for the purchase of this small part of the overall site, and drafted a letter for their Chairman, Sir Leslie Young, to sign, that would confirm this valuation. If he signed it, it was unlikely that any of our potential funders would agree to such a payment.

It was imperative to find a way to dissuade Leslie Young from signing, and Tony McGann found the way. He found out that his 'new friend' Chris Wates was also a good friend of Leslie Young. He also explained the land dilemma to a contact he had made in Liverpool, the Chairman of Vernons, the pools corporation. With the deadline drawing close, Tony received a phone call from the Chairman of Vernons on the Isle of Man, saying that Young was at a party with him and would Tony like to talk to him. Tony explained their problem with the extravagant valuation of the strip, and asked Young if he would be willing to meet with Chris Wates before he signed the letter. Young agreed, and McGann arranged for Wates to be in London the following week for the meeting. The two friends met, the letter was never signed, and British Waterways withdrew their demand. Another critical hurdle overcome.

Few people were aware at that time of Tony's increasing network of influential people. He uses the same straightforward approach with everyone and this seems to stand him in good stead. Whether it was an old woman on his doorstep needing help with her gas cooker, or a major national figure from whom he needed a favour, he treated them in the same way and they seemed to appreciate this. He has never changed his way of dealing with people, whoever they are – as Archbishop Worlock said of him, he has shown that he can, in Kipling's words, 'walk with princes – nor lose the common touch.'

Goal 2: securing the funds

With the option on the land secured, we then focused our attention on sources of funding. Again our extensive lobbying, described earlier, brought rewards. The Secretary of State for the Environment, Patrick Jenkin, decided to visit the area on 7 June 1984 to see for himself the housing conditions and to hear about our plans. Everyone realized that this was a very positive sign and a critical opportunity to convince Jenkin of the merits of the proposal and of the ability of the Eldonians to manage the new housing development once it was completed.

The visit was co-ordinated by Eric Sorensen of the Merseyside Task Force, who seemed to be impressed with the proposal. We were told that the minister would visit us in the morning and would then be given a tour of other parts of the city's housing by senior councillors in the afternoon. The *Liverpool Echo*, the main paper, saw the latter as a significant development as it was seen as a gesture of goodwill on the part of the minister, following repeated requests by the council.

The Eldonians decided that I should explain the background to the plans for the Tate & Lyle site as we escorted Patrick Jenkin up Burlington Street. As can be seen from the picture, he was flanked by me, Tony, Mickey Keating and Billy Little. I did my best to tell him about the developments at Portland Gardens, and moved on to the idea of how the remaining community wanted to build on the site, and would take responsibility for its design and management. I was not sure at the time just how much he was taking in, and always wondered afterwards if he was curious why the Eldonians were using a Canadian to explain their plans. I interviewed him twenty-three years later as part of this story and he told me that he thought I was a Scot!

When we arrived at the Eldonians' office in the tenements, they took over, again presented their exhibition and answered his many questions. At the end of some two hours he left. At the time, he did not give us any clear indication about what he thought about the plans, and certainly did not discuss funding. In fact, not even Tony asked him for a decision there and then! When I interviewed Lord Jenkin in June 2007, he recalled his reactions to this visit to Vauxhall to meet the Eldonians.

> My reaction was: this is some of the worst housing one had seen in Liverpool. And I could well understand the local community saying 'Look, we've got to do better; and we are determined to do this; we want to do it by ourselves, we don't want to be handed over to the City Council'. I think there was huge antipathy already by then, they'd *seen* what had happened. So, I realized that it was very bad housing, but I was convinced that these people had it within their sights to do something a great deal better, but they had to have a place to do it.

Putting our case to Secretary of State Patrick Jenkin. From the right: Mickey Keating, Tony McGann, Jenkin, Jack McBane

He also remembers being impressed with their determination and willingness to do what was necessary to get a result:

> I got the impression they were prepared to do business with me whereas a lot of the other people simply wanted to abuse. And I was very happy to respond to that. I felt I could do business with them. And I'm sure that the Task Force, Sorenson in particular, would have said 'You have a chance here to do something which really could make a difference'.

Of particular significance for the Secretary of State was that he clearly understood why this inner city community did not want to be moved out to the tower blocks on the edge of town:

> I visited one or two of those [blocks] that had been done earlier [in Liverpool] and they were *real* disaster areas. Under no circumstances was I *ever* going to sanction an increase in that movement out of the centre.

Patrick Jenkin meets more Eldonians. Left to right: Paul Orr, Billy Little, Margaret Clarke and Jo Somerset (from MIH)

> These were huge impersonal blocks, often with no effective hinterland for each block, no sense of ownership and no sense of involvement of any of the tenants. And of course, they became not only eyesores but also real social disasters. The people who moved there had left behind their communities and whatever they'd had in their neighbourhoods, and they were now faced with completely anonymous blocks of flats with no kind of community life at all. This happened not only in Liverpool but of course in a lot of other cities as well.

This impression was, most probably, passed on to English Estates and was a major influence in the Eldonians' continued progress in negotiations to develop the site.

It is now time to introduce Max Steinberg to the story. He is currently the Chief Executive of Elevate East Lancashire, which is one of the government's Housing Market Renewal Pathfinders. Max has been a supporter and friend of the Eldonians for over twenty-four years. He was born in Liver-

Tony McGann trying to 'close the deal' with Patrick Jenkin, now with a smile on his face

pool, and from 1978 to 2003 worked at the Housing Corporation, eventually becoming their Field Director for the north of England. He also worked as part of Michael Heseltine's team alongside the Merseyside Task Force in the early 1980s following the civil disturbances. As part of the Housing Corporation, Max was directly involved in the funding of a range of initiatives by the Eldonians. He is one of those professionals who was so impressed by the Eldonians that he became a long-standing supporter and friend. As with many of their friends, the Eldonians named a court after Max as their way of saying thank you.

Max recalls Michael Heseltine's interest in creating the thirty 'flagship projects' that would demonstrate how Liverpool could begin to reinvigorate itself. Towards the end of 1982 and during 1983, Max worked closely with colleagues within both the Housing Corporation and the Merseyside Task Force to get the viable projects 'on site'. He explained how, as these projects shaped up into programmes with costs and potential budgets, the government decided to use funds from existing national programmes to create what was known as the Merseyside Special Allocation. The funding for *housing* schemes within this Special Allocation was passed to the Housing Corporation, which was then responsible for delivering the schemes. The housing schemes included the Cathedral Precinct new-build development; Stockbridge Village at Cantril Farm; and the site at Tate & Lyle.

The funding issues were complicated because some of the sites for housing required considerable reclamation because of their previous industrial use. While the Housing Corporation's expertise was social housing and the issues concerned with costs and funding for schemes run by housing associations, it was not geared up for land reclamation. The land had to be decontaminated and the soil removed and disposed of. The Tate & Lyle site required over £2 million to make it safe. However, Michael Heseltine had anticipated this problem, as discussed earlier, with his Derelict Land Grant Programme. The negative value of the site would be removed through this intervention.

Max's memory of that time is that initially there were discussions on 'how to respond to the situation in the Vauxhall area, which would help the community and actually help redevelop an area that was clearly in severe distress'; but actual plans for some of the other special projects, for example the new housing at Cathedral Precinct, were more advanced. However, from 1981 to 1983, responding to the 'circumstances in Vauxhall' was increasingly on the agenda, not least because of the pressure on the government and the Housing Corporation from Liverpool leaders and from the Eldonians:

> There was a strong interest among a number of people in their future, and while it's well documented about the late Derek Worlock's and David Sheppard's interest, Tony's ability to charm and mesmerise Minister after Minister, official after official, and speak in a very persuasive and passionate way, came across very strongly.

This is, again, confirmation that our continuous campaign to present the issues to a wide range of people, including the Secretary of State, combined with the sheer power of our case, had a positive effect on those who were in a position to do something about it.

Max Steinberg offers his own perspective:

> I think it was about the fact that here is a group of people who feel that not only, in a sense, is their area potentially in eternal decline but actually the powers that be – and by that I mean primarily the city council – are somehow fundamentally against them. I think they were a

> community who had a strong feeling of being in dire adversity and then dug their heels in and said 'Enough is enough... we're going to fight and we're going to do it on our terms; we want a solution on *our* terms not your terms.'

At last, at the end of 1984 the funding for the Eldonian Village was approved in principle through the Housing Corporation's Special Merseyside Allocation. This was the decision for which so many people had worked hard. There was now a notional figure in the Housing Corporation's 1984/85 budget for both the land reclamation and the house building. Still to come was a protracted period of negotiations between the Eldonians, their architects and the Housing Corporation on the detail of the budget and the design of the scheme. And it was not until 1987, when the Housing Corporation approved the final costings, that we had a legally binding arrangement. But, for the likes of Tony, his neighbours, me and the other professionals, this was a binding commitment and a major milestone in the history of the Eldonians. Everyone believed that a way had been found to develop the village. And as Tony said 'As it turned out, the winner [of the ideas competition] got £6,000; the losers got £6 million!'

Phase 1 of the Eldonian Village: To the Finishing Post

12

A DANGER FOR ANY community on a long journey is the loss of momentum, the disappointment that every step takes so long and that there are so many hurdles to overcome. The challenge now was to keep moving forward as a whole community during the next eighteen months of negotiations with the Housing Corporation. The key elements of our strategy at this point were publicity and a programme of practical developments.

Publicity

Our first step was to proclaim from the rooftops that the in-principle funding approval from the Housing Corporation was incontrovertible evidence that the scheme would eventually happen. What led us to this risky decision?

If the site had been just another piece of land in a housing association's portfolio, nothing would have been announced publicly at this stage, because there was still some way to go before the scheme was formally approved. However, this was not 'just another piece of land'. The campaign to get this far had been very public and sometimes controversial. There were 145 families in Vauxhall whose future was hanging on this, and we had to maintain momentum, maintain optimism and keep the community together. So the community celebrated this as a major landmark, as proof that the village *was* going to be built.

Confidence was vital during this period, particularly in relation to Liverpool City Council. On their first scheme in Portland Gardens, the Eldonians had already experienced at first hand the new council's policy on housing developments – the new-build housing programme was to be municipal: owned, managed and maintained by the city council, with no place for housing cooperatives. Having destroyed their first co-op, the council set out to undermine the confidence of local people in the proposed village on the Tate & Lyle site by assuring them that it would not happen and by refusing planning consent for the change of use for the site, about which we will hear later.

George Evans, then working for the city council's Housing Department, recalls being given clear instructions in 1984 for dealing with the 145 families who were members of the Eldonian Housing Co-op and still living in the old tenements:

> We were advised that the co-op scheme would not be going ahead. We were called in – 'Forget what you've heard in the past, there'll be no new-build. Start off with the people from Vauxhall and get them back on track. Go and tell them that there's no co-op and tell them that if they want to move out, they can, but they better make their minds up quickly.'

'Them', of course, included Mr and Mrs Tony McGann. George continues:

> I remember Sheila, she was one of my Rehousing Assistants. She was tasked to go out and tell Tony McGann this, and she was terrified. She said 'I can't go and tell Tony that, you know what he's like, he'll blow up'. I rang up Tony and said 'Look, Sheila's coming out and another girl, to tell you. We've been told to tell you this.' Tony knew the score. So he got them in and Joan made them a cup of tea, probably a piece of toast, and he said 'I know why you're here, but I couldn't care less what you say; I'm not moving and you can tell that to Liverpool City Council; and neither is anyone else who's a member of this co-op, none of us are moving, so you'll have to demolish around us!' It was okay, we'd done our job, we'd gone out and we'd come back, and we'd said it.

Later on, when it was clear that members of the co-op were standing their ground, staff were told to step up the pressure. If any tenant was a member of the co-op, staff were to go and make them even better offers, including anywhere they wanted to live in council accommodation in the city. I recall witnessing one of these visits by Housing Department staff to an elderly lady who was in the co-op and who expected to be able to relocate to the new village across the road at Tate & Lyle. The young officer explained that she had a number of housing options on her list from which the elderly lady should choose. The lady said that she was staying and would be moving into the new co-op scheme in due course. The officer said that the co-op was not an option because it was not on her list, and asked her again. Again she received the same answer. Finally the officer said, in exasperation, that if the lady did not choose one of the options offered, she would put her into an old people's home somewhere. Although she was not known for being aggressive in any way, the lady replied, 'If you don't piss off, I'll put *you* in a fucking coma!'

A senior Labour councillor told Bishop Sheppard 'All they want is a good house. When we can offer them good housing, all that support for a co-operative will melt away.'[1] In the event most people turned down attractive rehousing offers from the council, and few moved. So the risky publicity strategy was working – people believed that the scheme would happen.

Practical developments

Confident public announcements would not be enough to maintain momentum if they were not accompanied by action to propel the Eldonians forward. The first step, therefore, was to establish the Eldonian Housing Cooperative in 1984. Tony McGann was its Chair, and a representative committee was drawn from the 145 families. It had an office in the flat in Eldon Street, and it appointed Bill Halsall as the architect to design the first phase of the village.

The second step was to begin work with the future residents on the design of their new homes, and on a programme of learning about how the housing co-op would actually work.

The design process

Bill Halsall, as the co-op's architect, led on the design process. Co-op members were invited to work alongside Bill, resulting in a core of around fifteen people, including Joan McGann – the design committee.

While Bill was aware that this process was part of the communal effort to keep people engaged, busy and positive during the period of negotiations, he was also aware of the positive aspects of having this length of time to devote

1 Sheppard and Worlock, *Better Together*, 208.

Members of the Housing Co-op committee outside their 'office'. Left to right: Margaret Dragonette, Margaret Clarke, Tony McGann and Margaret Campbell

to design. There was no need to rush people as they learned about it. Ideas had time to mature and to be discussed by a range of committees and groups, giving members a deep sense of ownership of the final result. As Margaret Dragonette, one of the co-op members, recalls:

> First of all we had to have a design, an outline of where the houses were going to be, where they were going to be placed and all that sort of stuff – so the design committee had the brief to come up with a layout. And Bill brought a base and little blocks and they played around with them. And each time they came up with a finished version they were always democratic, it was always brought back to the whole of the co-op. It wasn't just the committee that made the decision, it was always brought back to the general meeting.

The flat in Eldon Street became a base camp for everything that was going on, including the regular meetings, exhibitions and models, and examples of some of the building materials for the new houses.

The first step was to gather the details of the co-op families. After that Bill began to plan the different house types, for example, the number of bedrooms in the house. This was done through a series of meetings with the different house type groups, including those who would live in bungalows. The next step was to decide 'who lives where'. At that point, explains Bill,

> we had the design committee and a range of membership meetings where the model of the site had been developed and alternatives considered. This was how the basic shape of the village was agreed. And then the broad distribution of house types had been agreed. There was a sort of allocation policy that had been drawn up to decide what sizes of family could get what kind of house, and there was an 'extra bed space' rule whereby families were allowed an extra bed space capacity built in.

The next key stage in this design process was to allocate the actual plots where families were to live. This was difficult for the co-op members. Everybody's preference was to be close to Vauxhall Road, which was the main road at the 'front' of the scheme, rather than Love Lane, which backed onto an industrial area and the railway line. Bill realized that this issue was not going to be resolved easily through discussion among the members, so it was decided to use the club's bingo machine! Margaret Dragonette recalls it vividly:

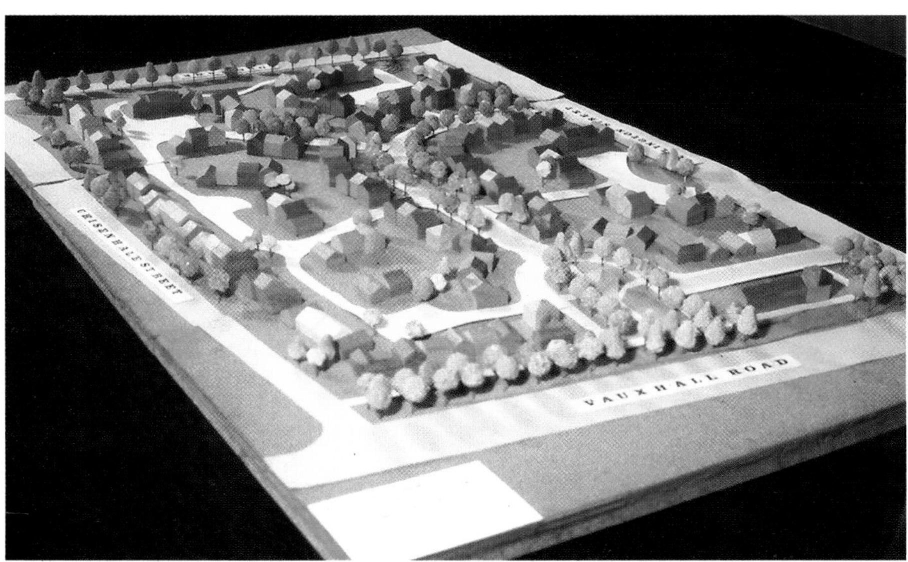

The model of Phase 1 that the design committee and Bill Halsall developed

> So we thought what's going to be the fairest, who's going to draw the numbers out? So we thought, Father Dunne, if you want to be sure of no cheating, get the priest involved! So we did it over a period of three days and three nights. We had a lot of people who wanted to be next door to each other. We did the bungalows first, and anyone who was in a bungalow, whose daughter or son was going to be next door to them, came on the first night. And they went in and they were given a number, and that number went into the bingo machine. Bill was there with all his gang, and we had a big map of the site. When a number was picked out – say it was my mother and grandmother because they wanted to live next door to each other – they went over to where Bill was, and they told him what type of property they had and where they wanted to live on the site. So Bill showed them on the map 'there's a house and bungalow next to each other', and you chose which one you wanted and your name was put on that plot.

Bill recalls how some members were keen to stay in a group:

> I particularly remember there were some people who had worked together in Tate & Lyle, that they wanted to go in a little group; and there were some family groups. They went up on a single number to try and get houses in a block or in a court.

Most people were placed satisfactorily through this process, but there was still a week or so after the allocations for people to swap with each other before they were finalized.

Bill found this 'bingo' event exciting because there was so much at stake for the local people. Most of the people living in the tenements had, by now, 'burned their bridges' with the city council by refusing the offers of rehousing. He felt that the model that they had made of the new scheme began to take on a special significance: 'The block model that then got stuck down as it were, became quite iconic in a way, it became what everybody related back to.' As Margaret said 'that was when people knew where they were going to live.'

It is easy to underestimate the importance of the commitment made by the two key professional organizations to the Eldonians during this period of uncertainty – Wilkinson, Hindle, Halsall & Lloyd Partnership through Bill Halsall, and Merseyside Improved Houses (Riverside Housing) through Barry Natton, its Chief Executive. Both Bill and Barry Natton were out on a limb during this time, due to the uncertainty of the funding. Despite this uncertainty, Barry continued to fund me to stay with the scheme; and Bill continued with his work, even though his practice was not being paid.

Preparing to run the cooperative

Alongside the design process, members began to learn about how to run a co-op and manage houses. This was made possible by Merseyside Improved Houses' decision in 1985 to commit further to the Eldonians. By this time I was only working on a part-time basis as I was now living in Sheffield. However, MIH appointed George Evans as my replacement to work with the Eldonians, specifically to prepare them for their new estate on the Tate & Lyle site.

For George this was a significant move in his career, as he had worked for many years within the structure of the local authority and was now going to work on a scheme that was not, at that time, guaranteed to happen. As a council officer responsible for housing in Vauxhall, he had been working with the Eldonians for nearly two years at this stage and remembers his decision to make the move:

> The more I worked with them, the more I was convinced that they were looking at it in the right way. They were looking at it in a way that was the future, in a way that made sense. I was convinced that empowerment rather than consultation was the way forward. I *had* to be convinced because at the time the people who were involved weren't academically superior to anyone else; they just had a belief in themselves that was hard to overcome. And when you see that belief in the light of some of the terrible housing conditions they were enduring and made to endure, then you've got to think – Yeah, if they can have that belief, then so can you.

At the request of the co-op committee, George ran a housing management programme for its members, running alongside Bill's design work. His aim was to help the group understand what was involved in managing a housing scheme. He helped them to develop policies and procedures that would serve them in the future, and he helped them to register the co-op with the Housing Corporation. His training programme included policies on the full range of basic housing management systems: a membership policy for admitting new people to the scheme; a way of allocating property; the administration of rents, repairs and maintenance; a tenancy agreement; accounts and so on.

A fact of life for the members of the co-op was the endless meetings. Although describing Portland Gardens, Rita Potter gives us a flavour of the impact of them on their daily lives:

> We used to come home from work and Tony would remind us, 'There's a meeting in the club at half past seven'. I didn't even get out of work till seven o'clock. We'd go straight to the meeting and wouldn't have a penny between us. When it was over, Tony would get us all a drink, or Paul Orr, or whoever's there. Soon I would say, 'I'm not sitting here without paying for a drink. Jane (who worked behind the bar), can we have trust?' She would agree and put our names on a piece of paper on the wall behind the bar. So on a Thursday we had to go straight from work with our wages and pay the bill, because sometimes we'd have meetings three times a week. I used to think, I've worked all week to have me wages gone on a bar bill! We used to tell our husbands, 'We're going to a meeting straight from work, – see you at two o'clock in the morning!' And we had overalls on, dancing away in the club!

So, as these two main programmes engaged co-op members for the next eighteen months, the negotiations continued involving members of the Eldonians, MIH, Councillor Paul Orr and Bill Halsall. Meetings were held with English Estates, the landowners; the Housing Corporation, the holders of the funds; the Merseyside Task Force, as the link to the government; and Liverpool City Council, as the planning authority. They were frequent and complicated, and no one today can accurately recall the exact sequence and content of them in any great detail. They concerned the reclamation of the site and its costs; the costs of the housing scheme; its design and layout; and the planning approval to change the site's designation from industrial to housing. By 1987 all but one of these issues were resolved. The Housing Corporation finally announced publicly the funding for the Eldonians' new scheme on the Tate & Lyle site, but it was not without a final drama.

The Planning Inquiry

The old site at Tate & Lyle had been used for industrial purposes for over 100 years. Although the land was owned by English Estates, it still required a change in status from industrial to housing land, and this involved an application to

Liverpool City Council. Of all the events in the long journey of the Eldonians from slum tenements to their new houses in their new village, this is the one that most people clearly remember. It is now part of their folklore.

In early 1985 the application for 'change of use' for the land was submitted to the council. In May the council refused the request. While most of the people who were involved with the scheme were not surprised by this decision, we were nonetheless very disappointed. We knew that this was the final hurdle that the council could place in the way of the scheme going ahead. The people of Vauxhall had stood up to the council; they had taken control of their local ward party to ensure that local people would represent them in future; they had publicly challenged the council's decision in 1983 to destroy the Portland Gardens co-op; and they had stood together against the attempts to undermine the Eldonian housing co-op. They were now paying dearly for their courage.

The reason given by the council for refusing a change of use for the land was the danger to health. The refusal letter cited the location of a number of small, long-established local industries that emitted fumes that could be hazardous to the health of people living near to them, namely on the Tate & Lyle site. These industries included a business that crushed bones from animals for the production of glue and an old tannery. As they had been established prior to the legislation that could have closed them down, there was nothing the council could do about them. The smells were undoubtedly unpleasant, although local people had put up with them for most of their lives and had become accustomed to them. At one level the council's objections could be seen as valid. However, the council itself had previously approved the construction of a junior school adjacent to the site and, of course, only three years earlier had submitted its own bid to the ideas competition, which included 150 houses on this same site. Surely the obvious course of action would have been to relocate these small industries rather than risk losing the opportunity to rehouse 145 families into new homes.

A meeting was organized between the Eldonians and their professional advisors and English Estates. The latter were, by this point, committed to the Eldonians' plans. They seemed to realize the David and Goliath dimensions of this struggle and they were impressed by the determination of these people who were living in such appalling conditions. The meeting decided to appeal against the council decision and to call for a Public Inquiry.

English planning law offers the right of appeal to an applicant if they are unhappy with the decision made by their local authority. The applicant may appeal to the Secretary of State and request a Public Inquiry. If this is successful, an independent Inspector is appointed to consider the appeal. In order to present their case and cross-examine the council, the applicant usually seeks legal planning advice. The Inspector will also visit the site and ask questions of the parties during this visit. Following the Public Inquiry, the Inspector prepares a formal report, including a recommendation that is sent to the Secretary of State for consideration and an announcement of the outcome of the appeal.

English Estates decided to take no risks with the Inquiry and told us to find the best planning QC in the country. None of us had any direct experience of planning inquiries or any contacts in this area. By strange coincidence, shortly afterwards I was travelling by train from London to Sheffield and struck up a conversation with a fellow traveller, who turned out to be a Planning Inspector! I explained our situation and asked his opinion about appropriate QCs to take our case in the upcoming Inquiry. Without hesitation, he recommended Jeremy Sullivan QC and said that in his view he was among the best. We contacted Sullivan, met him in his chambers at Gray's Inn in London and explained the background to the application and subsequent refusal by the council. His decision to represent us gave everyone considerable comfort.

The Inquiry took place in October 1985 and was held in the grand Central Library in the centre of Liverpool. It lasted for a day and the hall was full to capacity, mainly with members of the Eldonians. One of the day's memorable events was when Archbishop Worlock arrived to act as a witness for the Eldonians. The atmosphere throughout the proceedings had been very formal and followed a set procedure, including the Inspector sitting on a dais at the front of the hall. As the Archbishop entered this formal setting, the audience rose to give him a standing ovation. There was great laughter in which the Inspector joined. Archbishop Worlock spoke on behalf of the Eldonians, and his words have proved to be prophetic, as he recalls in *Better Together*:

> In the temporary courtroom in the City Library, which was filled for the occasion with applauding Eldonians, I assumed the mantle of a prophet as I testified on their behalf: 'I share the view of many that the next decade will see the further development of the riverside area bordering the Mersey. The work of reclamation, begun at the Garden Festival and the Albert Dock, will continue along the waterfront below Vauxhall. It

> would be an injustice if the present families in the Vauxhall community were to be denied the opportunity to share in the benefits of this facility.'[2]

The centrepiece of the Inquiry was when the council's Director of Public Health presented the council's case for refusing the application. He came forward and mounted a large map on a display board, covered with coloured dots and arrows. He spoke for some sixty minutes and his case consisted mainly of the number of complaints from the public over the years about the foul smells from the industries adjacent to the Tate & Lyle site. Each dot represented a specific address and the arrows represented the direction of the wind at the time of the complaint. He pointed out that, as could be seen from his map, the prevailing wind was from the southwest and therefore the site was in its direct line. The council, he explained, was concerned about the health of local people and that any proposal to build new houses on this site would put them at risk.

We were all taken aback by his presentation as no one had realized that such a record of complaints existed. Our man, Sullivan, sat quietly throughout the sixty minutes without asking any questions. The hall fell silent. When asked by the Inspector if he had any comments on the Director's presentation, Sullivan stepped forward, walked over to the large map, and asked the man from the council whether he would have concerns if the wind had been coming from the opposite direction. He replied that in this event, he would have no objections to the proposal. Sullivan then asked him whether he realized that his map was upside down. The Inspector and the embarrassed Director were among the few people in the hall not to collapse into hysterical laughter.

There followed a visit to the site and the offending industries after which the Inspector closed the formal proceedings to write her report. Within a month Kenneth Baker, the new Secretary of State for the Environment, announced that he had overturned the council's decision and that he was granting approval for the change of use for the site.

This was an enormous relief and an excuse for another large celebration in the old Jubilee Hall. There was also a service of thanksgiving in the church, led by Archbishop Worlock, and later a 'Festival on Sand' on site. Derek Worlock wrote a very moving account of the thanksgiving service:

2 Sheppard and Worlock, *Better Together*, 211.

> A great celebration took place in the packed church in Eldon Street in mid-November. Then in pouring rain a procession formed to go, as it were in pilgrimage, to the site which was to be the cherished Eldonian Village. Elderly housebound people were brought in local taxis and vans to witness the scene of their dreams. Schoolchildren lined the route, waving their flags. Perhaps the most remarkable feature of this act of thanksgiving for the success which had marked the solidarity and perseverance of the local people, was the wording of the great banner across the road. In this area in the heart of Scotland Road, where sectarian bitterness was for so many years at its worst, banners across the street and slogans in the windows had always been a familiar sight. The occasion of the breaking of the ground for the Eldonian Housing Co-operative was no exception. But the content of the slogan said much for the different spirit. Across the street, in the windows and on the back of the service booklet, the message was plain: 'Our thanks to Archbishop Derek, to Bishop David and to all our friends. WE DID IT BETTER TOGETHER'. The context and the wording of the slogan itself seemed to provide us with the right title for this book.[3]

As Tony puts it today, the final result was 'game, set, match and championship to the Eldonians'. The last major hurdle had been overcome.

On site at last

From the end of the Planning Inquiry to the first person moving into the Eldonian Village in July 1988 was just under three years. Along the way there were still practical hurdles to overcome, but the goal was clearly in sight. One such hurdle was the issue of Parker Morris space standards in housing. Since 1961 the national standard for publicly funded houses was known as Parker Morris. Throughout the 1980s the Conservative government had legislated for strict control of all local authority finance and, in 1980, abolished the Parker Morris standard, replacing it with a value-for-money formula, the effect of which was a smaller house. The Eldonians had asked Bill Halsall to use the Parker Morris standards for their new houses, and argued strongly with the Task Force and Housing Corporation to retain them. Bill remembers a time very close to putting the scheme out to tender for construction when he and Tony were summoned to the Task Force's office and instructed to reduce all

3 Sheppard and Worlock, *Better Together*, 211.

The 'desert' in the middle of Vauxhall and site for the Festival on Sand

Bishop Sheppard and Archbishop Worlock lay the first bricks with a relieved-looking Bill Halsall

145 houses to the new size – which meant a 10 per cent cut – and to get the final costs within a new budget. If he could not do this, there would be no scheme. After many more late hours, Bill and his colleagues achieved the new size, and the scheme was ready to go out to tender for construction.

In September 1987 construction of Phase 1 began, and in September 1988 David Trippier, the Minister for Housing, Inner Cities and Construction, presented the keys to Mrs Ann Bland and her family, the first occupants of the Eldonian Village. The last family to move in was the McGanns in September 1989. On 3 May 1989 Prince Charles formally opened the Eldonian Village. The *Liverpool Echo* was there to report on the occasion:

> The prince spoke of how 'blunt speaking' like that employed by Mr McGann was needed from time to time. And he recalled how the Eldonians' chairman had invited him to the opening and put a postscript to his letter saying: 'Don't be late!' Men and women through the power of their own personalities could achieve more than millions spent by committees, he said. 'People should see for themselves what has been

David Trippier presents Ann Bland with the key to the first house in the village

> achieved here and take it back to their own areas. You have set a great example and now people have a model to follow.'[4]

The photograph of Prince Charles visiting the home of Maureen McGuinness in 1989 captures the continuity of community in this neighbourhood. Standing with Maureen is her daughter, Sharon, and her grandson, Francis. Sharon now has her own home in the village, and her son Francis is twenty-two and is training as an apprentice gas fitter with the Eldonian Group. He and his partner have been on the waiting list for a home in the village for the last two years.

Moving into their new homes was a momentous time for the Eldonians. Tony McGann says:

4 *Liverpool Echo*, 4 May 1989, 13.

Prince Charles at the opening of the village, accompanied by Bill Halsall while visiting Maureen McGuinness, her daughter Sharon, and grandson Francis

The happy families celebrating their new homes

> Once people got on the site, the funny thing about it, they were talking about it as their holidays! And some people were saying 'We don't believe this'; they were waiting for it to end – 'We've got to go home in two weeks time!' And they still say it now, after all these years 'I still think I'm on me holidays here, Tony!' People just couldn't believe it; so happy; they were all kept together, they were all neighbours that were brought up with one another, the same families.

The original plan for Phase 1 included provision of new shops at the front of the village along Vauxhall Road, an idea from the submission to English Estates. Despite the desperate need for new shops in the area, however, it proved impossible to secure the funding to build them. Unfortunately, most funders at that time had no discretion to widen the purposes for which grants could be used. Housing funds, for example, could only be used for housing, not shops. Never ones to be defeated by a setback, the Eldonians with Bill Halsall developed instead the idea of creating a home for thirty frail and elderly people on this land.

Tony took the idea to Max Steinberg at the Housing Corporation who

The Rt. Hon. David Trippier at the opening of Eldonian House. Margaret Jackson is on his left.

A proud Tony McGann

saw the sense of such a scheme as it went to the heart of what the Eldonians stood for: keeping the community together. Max went to the Department of the Environment in London to convince them of the scheme's merits; and some four weeks after this visit, Chris Patten, the new Secretary of State for the Environment, visited the village and announced the funds for the frail and elderly scheme.

Once again Riverside Housing worked closely with the Eldonians on this project and agreed to own and manage it until the Eldonians purchased it back from them some years later. Today it is owned and managed by the Community Based Housing Association. The home, called Eldonian House, cost £1m and was opened in October 1991 by David Trippier, by then the Minister of State for the Environment and Countryside.

The layout of the village was the result of Bill Halsall's work with the residents' design committee. It has a central core road through the middle of the scheme, called Eldonian Way, with five courts off it. The housing co-op committee named the five courts after people they regarded as critical to the development of the whole scheme. There are 145 houses and bungalows. No two houses are the same because each family was able to shape the interior of their new home. In fact, there are 28 different house types on the site.

Upon completion of the first phase of the village, the Eldonians appointed Riverside Housing to assist them with its management. George Evans described this arrangement:

> The Eldonians retained ownership and control. Some of that control was devolved through a management agreement with Riverside Housing. A list of responsibilities, a contract if you like, was drawn up between both parties whereby a task was identified and apportioned.

The arrangement was based on the policies and procedures that had been developed and agreed by the Eldonians, through the work that George had done with them. Riverside Housing acted as an agent whereby it carried out the practical work such as repairs, following an instruction from their client. Gradually management was passed over to the Eldonians' own organization, the Community-Based Housing Association, and George joined them as its first employee in 1993, as Director of Housing.

Home, sweet home

I spoke to a number of residents who have lived in Phase 1 since it was completed in 1989. I asked about how it felt to move into the village, and how they feel about living there today. All spoke about the extraordinary transformation of their lives, and all agree on the key aspects of the village that made it such a success and keeps it that way today.

Frank Brady and his family felt as though they had moved to Aigburth (an attractive suburb of the city) when they first moved in. Linda Coburn and her young family moved from a flat in the tenements that was cold and damp. Her fondest early memory was the new gas fire and central heating. Lynn Burke was most impressed with the sense of space both within their house and outside; while Marie Ryan remembers that she and her six closest neighbours all moved together into Paul Orr Court.

Community safety has become a major issue across the UK, with few inner-city urban places feeling safe to their residents today. In contrast, the Eldonian residents all agree about how safe the village was for their young children growing up, and how safe they still feel within the village today. They acknowledge that the design of the village, with its courts, has been a major

The Eldonian Way looking back at Our Lady's Church

Phase 1: looking out from Jack McBane Court

factor in this. Bill Halsall and his design group took the idea of courts from the old tenements, with their central area in full view of all the decks. In both cases, adults are able to keep a watch on what goes on, and their children can play in safety. 'Full credit to the architect for this', said Frank Brady. He also points out that in this community and in the communities nearby there are no gangs of young people causing trouble. He believes that this is partly because they all go to the same schools, and that the village encourages openness and co-operation. Linda Coburn describes the village as 'a nice, clean, warm place for kids to grow up': 'My kids have done well living here, as they felt good about growing up here. They are going to University next year.'

We also talked about the condition of the village today and again they all agree that it looks as good today as the day they moved in, eighteen years ago. There must be few housing estates in the UK that could make this same claim. Both Frank and Linda said that people feel that they own the village and so have a sense of personal responsibility to keep it looking as it does. Frank told me that, in eighteen years, he has never seen graffiti anywhere in the village. They all acknowledge that it is this ownership of their community that most sets the village apart from council estates. Frank commented on how low-income families would never have been able to purchase housing of

Phase 1: An example of the different house types

this quality, so close to the centre of the city. Linda said, 'We feel we own the village, so we take pride in it and everyone wants to keep it nice.'

And to what do they attribute all of this? 'Strong leadership', said Frank. 'Any sign of trouble is nipped in the bud. Nothing is left to get worse. I give

Phase 1: Evidence of the pride and care of the people who live here

full credit to the people who manage the village.' Linda explained that 'the CBHA are good to deal with; they listen and they get things done. Antisocial behaviour is not tolerated.'

As for living anywhere else, Marie Ryan told me, 'Moving to the village was the best thing we ever did. We could have moved out to God knows where, like many did, and they lived to regret it.' She hopes to live in the village until she dies. Finally, Frank Brady sums it up for them all: 'I'm made up living here.'

Conclusion

It was a roller-coaster ride for the Eldonians and their team of professionals from 1981, when Tate & Lyle closed their sugar refinery, to September 1988 when Ann Bland and her family moved in to their new home in the Eldonian Village. At any point during these seven years the members of this community or their advisors could have abandoned the struggle to create a new neighbourhood. There were many times when their commitment was put to the test, as explained in the story, and there were many periods of doubt and delay when it was not certain that the scheme would go ahead. Lined up against these problems and delays was a group of people, both local people and outside advisors, who had an enormous amount of courage, charm, stubbornness, wit and many good friends. The Eldonians had a simple idea and its strength and righteousness was hard to resist. Many of the key officials from that period have since confirmed this, as can be seen in the Tributes in Appendix 2.

There were many people all over Liverpool during the 1980s who grew to admire the determination and courage of these people. And for good reason. First, it took seven years of dogged campaigning and sheer hard work; secondly, the residents were in the highest category of housing need and they chose to remain in their decaying property throughout this time; thirdly, although it was coincidental that a site came empty when it did, they had the ingenuity to realize its potential. They stayed the course when most of the surrounding neighbourhoods gave in to the city council and allowed their communities to be destroyed.

When any community battles as hard and doggedly as the Eldonians, it is almost inevitable that some misconceptions about them will arise and circulate. One of the most hurtful was the assertion that they benefited at the direct expense of other equally needy communities in Liverpool. After the Planning

Inquiry, a rumour took hold that the Eldonians had 'jumped the queue' by manipulating the government to fund them at the expense of the city council. It is time to put to rest this long-standing misconception. On the first point, the Eldonians were at the front of the queue, living in a slum clearance area, which is why the council had offered them rehousing in the first place.

On the second point, regarding the funding, Michael Parkinson, while not commenting on the Eldonians themselves, appears to confirm the view that the funding of mixed housing schemes at the time was at the expense of the council. In *Liverpool on the Brink* he writes that Patrick Jenkin, as Secretary of State, tried and failed to get the council to agree to a mixed approach to building new housing, including housing associations and housing co-ops. He continues:

> It was only because of Labour's intransigence on its municipal housing strategy that the cuts in its housing budget were made. The approximate amount that was taken from the Labour council's housing budget, £9m, was later added to the Housing Corporation's budget for housing in Liverpool, to promote the work of housing associations and diversify housing provision in the city.[5]

However, Max Steinberg today confirms that the funds for all the 30 regeneration projects in Merseyside came from the Merseyside Special Allocation, which was top-sliced from national not local programmes. And, of course, just one of these involved the Eldonians, namely, the Tate & Lyle site.

Finally, it is appropriate that the last words on the most important period of their history should be Tony McGann's:

> I *always* believed that it was going to happen, even though it was against all the odds. If I'd have thought any other way I would have just rolled over; so I kept in my mind 'it's going to happen'. And I think that's what kept me going. I always believed that it was going to be a long, long battle; it was going to be an endurance test, and I set myself up for it. It gave me something to aim for as well. And the bottom line for me was, I've always believed in trying to help people. I was looking out for everyone else around here, to keep the community together, a decent job to go to, a safe place to live, and obviously a proper education for our children. And we've achieved most of that.

5 Parkinson, *Liverpool on the Brink*, 130.

Key development phases for the Tate & Lyle site from reclamation to completion of Phase 1 of the Eldonian Village

- 1981: Tate & Lyle sugar refinery closed
- 1982: ideas competition for the Tate & Lyle site – A Self-Regenerating Community
- March 1984: English Estates offered the site to the Eldonian Housing Cooperative
- November 1985: Planning approval granted, and design of the houses began
- December 1985: Feasibility study into the state of the land began
- March 1986: Feasibility study completed, finding considerable contaminates and tarwells from previous commercial use of the site
- April 1986: Cost of proposed reclamation works estimated at £2.2m
- December 1986: Wimpey Construction commenced reclamation works – dumping around 150,000m^3 of sand on the site; dredging sand from the River Mersey, and raising the level of the site some three metres
- January 1987: Eldonian Housing Cooperative purchased the site of twelve acres from English Estates
- February 1987: Detailed Planning Consent
- August 1987: Reclamation works completed
- September 1987: Construction of the Eldonian Village began
- September 1988: First family moved in to their new house

Phase 2 of the Eldonian Village: Consolidation

13

THIS IS THE FINAL chapter in the story leading up to the Eldonians today. As we have seen in Chapter 1, they have continued to develop and change to meet new challenges and circumstances to the present day, but these subsequent achievements have been in a different context – from the position of an established, well-respected, successful organization, no longer fighting for recognition every step of the way. In this chapter we see the beginnings of that different context, and their implications for the Eldonians.

The completion of Phase 1 brought a wide range of benefits. First and foremost they now had some of the best public housing in the country, which was 'tailor made' by and for the families that lived in it. For the first time in their lives all of the 145 families from the tenements on Burlington and Eldon Streets had houses with stairs and gardens, and with direct access to the street on which they lived. This was the 'Promised Land', and for some time many of them could not believe it; it felt like a holiday from which they would have to return.

Secondly, they had a stronger self-confidence – their long-standing commitment to this neighbourhood was confirmed. As we have seen throughout the story to date, these people were no 'blushing brides'. They knew how to stand their ground, whether to a council officer offering 'new' housing, or to the local Catholic Church offering a new structure for the parishes. Phase 1 of the Eldonian Village affirmed their belief and gave them a sense of pride, and this was to be a solid platform for further developments.

Thirdly, they now had enormous credibility in Liverpool, among major organizations on Merseyside, and at senior levels in the government. The government and regional bodies became proactive in wanting to work with them to help take forward their plans. They saw a community that believed in itself and had proved that it could put into practice its dreams, and they wished to be part of this emerging success story.

Fourthly, their achievements had begun to make their neighbourhood attractive as a residential area. Earlier in the book I described the Eldonians as an 'anchor' for this part of Liverpool. As the city council wanted to demolish most of the housing, with no plans for rebuild, and all major industry had gone, it is likely the area would now be light industrial or commercial. By refusing to move and achieving the first phase of the village, the Eldonians saved the area and offered hope to those who wanted to return from the outskirts of the city.

Finally, their success gave them the energy to revisit their plans from the ideas competition: A Self-Regenerating Community. The Eldonians, and in particular Tony McGann, were ready to go forward with the work to consolidate their new neighbourhood. Their plans included more new homes for families and elderly people, local facilities for sports and social activities, training and job creation, an office for the Eldonian organizations, a nursery for local children and a complete refurbishment of the Leeds/Liverpool canal on their site.

Phase 2 of the village: reaching out

The new housing was both successful and popular, but the Eldonians already knew that more social housing was required. There were the people living locally, just outside the Eldonian Village, in poor conditions – young families and elderly people living in high-rise blocks with unreliable lifts, and fearful about thieves and drug addicts outside their doors. There were former residents of the Vauxhall area who now desperately wanted to return and be part of this new neighbourhood. And there was an increasing demand from the children of the families on Phase 1, who, as they grew up, would need to have their own homes. As George Evans explains:

> Even though Phase 1 was a success and was running very well, we always felt there was a need for something else because the population of Phase 1 was middle-aged to elderly. It was made up of those people who had

Tony McGann and Max Steinberg

> come from the tenements in Eldon or Burlington Streets, and they were actually middle-aged when they lived there. There were very few young families; and all the people who were living in Phase 1 had grown up as part of the co-op. We realized that there was a great need to bring young people back into the area. In fact, if young people meant the children of the people who were already there, great. Otherwise those young people would have to move away from the area, and that would have meant closing the school and the decline of the church.

The Eldonian approach to this requirement for more social housing illustrated their new status. Take the group of 15 elderly people left in a nearby, almost abandoned high-rise block, Sheehan Heights. They approached the Eldonians asking for help to find a way to build 15 new houses in the area. Tony took this challenge on board, in the same manner as he solved the crisis of the 'earthquakes': 'I'll look into it, luv'. But this time he was knowledgeable about funding sources and processes, and he was also confident of a respectful and sympathetic ear in the organizations that could help. He approached the Housing Corporation and before long funding was approved, including a loan, for the Eldonians to build a 15-unit scheme for their elderly neighbours. The new St Gerard Close included houses, flats and bungalows and was, appropriately, opened by Tony McGann on 20 July 1990. Today it is owned and managed by the Eldonian Community Based Housing Association, and is as successful as all their other housing projects.

Their approach to their main social housing priority – another 150 houses, largely for young people and families – equally illustrates their new confidence and status. All the critical agencies stepped into line to help them – the Housing Corporation, where they had a strong supporter in Max Steinberg; the Merseyside Development Corporation which now wanted to be an active partner in future developments; and other major housing associations in the city which wanted to have a presence in an area that previously had featured no housing association schemes. This development became known as Phase 2, and was built on the remaining land on the Tate & Lyle site, and adjoining land owned by the Merseyside Development Corporation. So how did it come about?

The Housing Corporation

First, once again Max Steinberg at the Housing Corporation played a central role in the approval of funds. He recalled the events that led up to this and the factors that influenced the decisions:

> First of all, Phase 1 was regarded as being exceptionally well delivered and attractive. It ticked all the right boxes in terms of what people regarded as successful development. And increasingly, by that stage, there was increased awareness of how tenants and residents should get involved in this next phase as they had in the first phase. There was a clear case being articulated by Tony. I remember having several meetings with him about the demand that was being created by the predicted success of Phase 1. A start had been made, and the community wanted to further consolidate it with Phase 2.

For Max, there was another factor at play here, one that was critical at the time, and still is today – the issue of investing not just in housing but in neighbourhoods, and consolidating that investment. If investment is spread too thinly, its impact on a neighbourhood will be minimal and temporary. There needs to be a level of investment that will ensure the sustainable transformation of a place. As a key player in deciding the Housing Corporation's spend on Merseyside in the 1980s and 1990s, Max became convinced that although there was huge pressure in the city for investing elsewhere – and they were investing in other places – they had to keep investing in this area:

> I reminded myself that we took a decision about the frail elderly scheme (Eldonian House) and we took the right decision. We took the decision about the development at St Gerard Close, and again, we took the right decision. And finally there was the strong reputation of the Eldonian organization, the quality of housing it produced, for the way it managed that housing, and for their attention to detail. They were very keen to respond to the opportunity they'd been given – so much so that if people were involved in anti-social behaviour, or in drugs, that threatened their position in the organization. That kind of agenda was being developed well before it was formalized in government policy.

Today, it seems the government has learned this key point about the value of sustained investment and building on success. It has taken a long-term view in neighbourhood investment through its Housing Market Renewal Programme. Ironically, Max went on to become the Chief Executive of one of these initiatives in East Lancashire.

The government

Such was the status and reputation of the Eldonians by this time that in 1989 Margaret Thatcher, the Prime Minister, decided to make a private visit to see for herself. It is likely that her Secretaries of State for the Environment, including Patrick Jenkin and Chris Patten, had kept her informed of the Eldonians' progress.

It would be an understatement to say that Thatcher was unpopular in Liverpool, which had suffered so much from the industrial decline of the area and the considerable increase in unemployment. Many people were also incensed by the insensitivity of one of her Cabinet members, Norman Tebbitt, telling the unemployed they 'should get on their bikes and look for work'. As Michael Heseltine said in his interview for this book, 'the fact that there were no jobs anyway to go to, and they couldn't afford bikes, was neither here nor there!'

The day Thatcher arrived to visit the site coincided with the closure of yet another large manufacturer on Merseyside, the Birds Eye factory in Kirkby. So while she was being shown around the village, there were protestors along Vauxhall Road chanting, 'Maggie, Maggie, Maggie, Out, Out, Out.' However,

Prime Minister Margaret Thatcher hearing about new plans from Tony

The visit by Michael (now Lord) Heseltine and the Rt. Hon. Kenneth Clarke to discuss the new MDC boundary. Julie Lackey is on the left.

Tony was not going to be deflected from his objectives for the day – to impress on her the success of the scheme and, therefore, the wisdom of investing further in Phase 2.

As they did for all VIP visits, the Eldonians updated their exhibition and gave the Prime Minister a presentation on their new plans for continuing with their 'Self-Regenerating Community'. These plans for new houses required government approval to extend the boundaries of the Merseyside Development Corporation to include the docks in north Liverpool and the Vauxhall area. This was critical to the Eldonians, as the MDC had powers to approve its own planning developments – thus bypassing the city council – and it would provide them with direct access to government funding. They arranged for Archbishop Derek Worlock to be there with them to add more weight to their proposals, as he was by this time in regular touch with the Secretary of State, and indeed with the Prime Minister, about the wider issues facing Merseyside.

Tony and Max Steinberg accompanied her on a tour of the village. She gave nothing away on the day about her future intentions for assisting the Eldonians with their long-term plans, but they did not have to wait long before the first dividends of the visit came good. Within four months, Tony was invited to a private dinner with the Prime Minister at 10 Downing Street. He recalls that, upon arrival at 10 Downing Street, one of her 'minders' told him that he was not to ask her for money. His reply was equally to the point: 'What *else* am I here for?' He obeyed the instruction, but as soon as she asked her guests to tell her what they thought was needed to make communities successful and to keep them that way, he leapt in – and took the opportunity to reinforce all that she had seen and heard on her visit to Liverpool.

The Merseyside Development Corporation

The MDC was the third critical part of the jigsaw – they owned part of the land that the Eldonians needed to build their 150 houses. As an agency accountable to the government, the MDC was sympathetic to the government's funding policies in this part of Liverpool, but it required an amendment to the legislation to extend its boundaries to include the land for Phase 2.

In previous years such an obstacle might have seemed insurmountable to the Eldonians, but by 1989 the MDC was as keen to be part of the development as was the Housing Corporation. And, as we have seen before, the Tony McGann factor was key. The senior staff and Chairman of the MDC had also been 'charmed and disarmed' by him over the years. He recalls arriving at meetings with staff at the MDC, to hear the call go around the offices: 'Put your wallets and purses away, here comes Tony McGann!'

Max Steinberg summarizes the factors that led to the announcement of the funds for Phase 2:

> In my view there were three factors. It was the Development Corporation's decision to extend their boundaries, the perceived success that Phase 1 was clearly going to be, and finally the pressure that Tony was able to bring for further investment in the community. At that time I am clear that there was still a strong appetite [within the government] to show that things could be achieved in a different way if organizations chose to operate within the system. I think the government was very keen to support that, and all these factors led to the proposals for Phase 2 being further incorporated into the Special Merseyside Allocations.

And so another 150 new houses for rent were developed on the land north of Phase 1. Work commenced in 1993, was completed in 1996, and the new scheme was once again opened by Prince Charles in December of that year.

Tony McGann and Prince Charles have been friends from the 1980s, and have often shared platforms at conferences talking about their commitment to urban regeneration. As we have seen, Prince Charles formally opened the Eldonian Village in 1989. Opening Phase 2 of the village in 1996, he spoke of his admiration for the achievements of the Eldonians and, in particular, their leader, Tony McGann:

> What a real pleasure to come back again to the Eldonians after I was here in 1992, and for me the enjoyment is to come back at regular intervals and to see how much you have been developing each stage further and further, much to my astonishment...
>
> Tony McGann says how difficult it is to get these sorts of projects off the ground... I, as he says, have been trying to form partnerships and encourage all kinds of projects in different parts of the country, but Tony McGann is one of those rare people who can actually make these things happen much quicker it seems to me than almost anybody else...
>
> I can imagine how many moments of anxiety, aspiration, frustration you've all had over the years... What you see now outside here and in here... is a great tribute to all your energy and determination and enthu-

Phase 2: The new houses alongside the canal

Phase 2 houses

> siasm and never taking no for an answer – and of course, Tony McGann is the great exponent of the art of never taking no for an answer. His other great gift is being able to create these developments and projects, which at the same time not only create jobs but also seem to be in some remarkable way self-financing and self-perpetuating, and this is again a great secret which isn't easy to achieve, something which is sustainable in the long term.
>
> I … congratulate him most warmly and all the committee, and all those I know who have worked … in transforming this entire area into something really encouraging and … something that … makes people's lives infinitely more worthwhile.
>
> I can only wish you every possible success and thank you all again for the wonderfully warm welcome that you always give me whenever I come to the Eldonians.

The total cost of Phase 2, including land reclamation, was £7m in the form of a £5.5m grant from the Housing Corporation to the Eldonian CBHA, and a loan of £1.5m from the Co-op Bank. As predicted, many of the new people for Phase 2 were the children of families living in the first phase, and other young families from around the area. Over 300 families applied and the CBHA staff interviewed all of them.

Once again, Bill Halsall and his firm were used to design the houses and their layout. He is very proud of the result, and with good reason. He describes the new development as a 'punctuated scheme' – a development that people would be able to look into from Vauxhall Road. He was also keen to incorporate the canal, which was in the past a bathing facility – Tate & Lyle used to deposit hot water from their manufacturing process in the canal, providing local children with their own 'Turkish bath'. However, this was a controversial idea, as some people recalled the tragic drowning of a local youth, and others regarded the canal as a 'backwater'. By negotiation, he allayed their concerns, providing railings and a gate, and today the canal is the centrepiece of the village.

Boys swimming in the Leeds/Liverpool canal c.1890

The Annual Canal Boat Festival, with the Village Hall in the background

Private investors

A landmark for the Eldonians, and a clear indication of their impact on their neighbourhood, was the decision of private house builders to invest in new houses for sale in the area – an inconceivable development a few years before. How did this come about?

At the same time as they focused on new *social* housing, the Eldonians also began to look forward to a village offering a range of tenures. As prosperity rose in the area they realized, as Michael Heseltine had anticipated back in 1981, that the next generation of residents might want to buy a house or flat and new home-buyers might be attracted to the village. As Phase 2 of the social housing was underway, they began to initiate discussions with private house builders to attract them to invest in new houses for sale in the area. The first site they offered was Burlington Street, where Tony McGann and his family had once lived in the tenements. He and I spoke about the idea

New private homes at Eldon Wharf

and I put them in touch with a contact I had at Wimpey Homes. As Wimpey were also considering development in the inner cities, they soon met with the Eldonians. The outcome was the first new-build houses for sale in Vauxhall since anyone could remember. The new houses sold as soon as they were built and they are still popular today.

The Wimpey development sent out a strong message about the stability of this emerging new community, and other house builders would soon follow their example. The following account by George Evans demonstrates this. On completion of Phase 2 the Eldonians were approached by another developer wanting to build accommodation for sale on land adjacent to the village:

> The first thing they did was ask if they could use our name to help sell the properties because we'd built such a reputation – the Eldonians stood for good quality, no drugs, well managed, clean, tidy... So we allowed them to call it 'Eldon Wharf', by the canal, based on our name. They put it up, and their selling jargon was 'New build for sale, Eldon Wharf, close to the world-renowned Eldonian Village'!

New scale, new structures, new initiatives

Up to the completion of Phase 1 and its initial management through Riverside Housing, the formal Eldonian structure was that of a housing cooperative. This was appropriate to their needs at the time, but by the late 1980s it was a structure that was limiting their potential. Consolidation required new structures both to maintain existing achievements and to move into non-housing initiatives. So, between the late 1980s and the early 1990s, the new structures, set out in Chapter 1, were established – the overarching Eldonian Community Trust, the Eldonian Development Trust, which later became the Eldonian Group, and the Community Based Housing Association. This would enable the Eldonians to continue to expand their activities into all those areas beyond housing that are essential to a sustainable community – education, leisure, health and sports facilities, and training schemes and employment for local people – as set out in their bid in 1982 for 'A Self-Regenerating Community'. The resulting schemes and facilities are described in Chapter 1. Each of them was achieved, thanks mainly to the Eldonians' ingenuity and to the fact that their reputation went before them.

Margaret Jackson, a landscape architect and Community Projects Manager with Liverpool Housing Trust, first met the Eldonians in the mid-1980s, and like all the professionals who came to work for them, was attracted to them:

> They were very determined, articulate, very clever, politically savvy, enjoyed a laugh and suffered no fools, as they could see through anybody who was just a front. They were very astute people. To work with a group of people like that was something I wanted to do. I was really up for the challenge.

She and Christine Bailey initially shared the post of the first Development Manager of the Eldonian Development Trust, although Margaret went on to lead on the Trust's various physical and economic development projects for ten years. She saw her role as trying to translate the aspirations of the community – to provide both facilities and employment – into what might be possible on the ground. In her time the nursery, the offices, the village hall and the sports facilities were all established, along with a number of training, employment and health related projects. So how did the Eldonians put these later schemes together? Below are some examples:

The children's nursery

This was part of the Eldonians 'cradle-to-grave' approach to neighbourhood regeneration. They felt that they would not receive support from the local authority to run such a facility, so they had to look at ways in which a nursery could be self-financing. As Margaret explains:

> There were a number of hard decisions that had to be made to do this – if it was to be self-financing, it couldn't just be open to local people. We did a Business Plan and realized that the fees would be £80/£85 a week. And that was, in 1993, serious money. We felt that if we could get some places for local children, as well as create local training and job opportunities, then it would be worth doing.

In the true entrepreneurial spirit of the Eldonians, Margaret approached the Littlewoods organization, a large mail order/retail business. She discovered that they were also exploring sites for a nursery for their own staff, and so invited them to form a joint venture. Littlewoods put in 50 per cent of the capital. She then approached the Merseyside Development Corporation which now had such confidence in the Eldonians that they agreed to fund the other 50 per cent, to fund the reclamation of the land for the new building, and to transfer the land to the Eldonians. But what of providing affordable places for local children? Margaret explains:

> The deal was that Littlewoods would be allocated a certain number of places at an agreed rate. And they also managed to get the Health and Safety Executive to buy a certain number of guaranteed places at a higher rate, because they hadn't put any capital in. And on that basis, we were able to subsidize some community places!

In 1994 the Eldonwoods Nursery opened with 50 places for children aged from three months to five years. Why Eldonwoods? A local boy coined the word by combining Eldonian and Littlewoods, of course! The nursery continues to be a highly successful enterprise, run by local people, serving residents and businesses, and with profits that go back to the organization. The Eldonians now own the business outright, and it is now called 'Kids Unlimited'.

A village hall

As explained earlier, the people around Vauxhall used the old Jubilee Hall on Burlington Street for over seventy-five years as their 'local' and social club. It was built originally as a nonconformist chapel but had fallen into disuse. It was re-opened in 1896 as a Temperance Hall by Monsignor Nugent, with the funds from a public subscription in his honour, to celebrate his Golden Jubilee as a priest. While old Mgr Nugent may have had good intentions in trying to keep the locals from the 'evil drink', it was all to no avail. By the turn of the century, the hall was sold to Our Lady's parish as a social club. The hall had a bar upstairs for shows at weekends, and a bar in the cellar. It was one of the ugliest buildings in Liverpool, described by Tony McGann, its manager, as the only drinking hole in the city 'where you wiped your feet *after* you walked out!' Despite this, it was the centre of the community and played an important role in everyone's life. As Rita Potter puts it: 'the old club used to stink – and when I say stink, it was stinking!! – but oh, we enjoyed it more than anything'.

By the late 1980s, however, the old club was beyond restoration and would not do as the social centre for the new village. It was demolished along with the condemned tenements on Burlington Street. People needed a new place to fill the gap, and it was to the Development Trust and Margaret Jackson that Tony turned for a solution.

A site had been identified at the head of the canal and in the centre of the village. All that was now required was a design, the funds to build it, a contractor, the materials, and the fixtures and fittings. For most neighbourhood organizations, this would have been insurmountable. But the Eldonians had come too far to be put off by such a challenge.

Tony and Margaret worked together and came up with a cocktail of solutions. First, they asked Bill Halsall to design the building for nothing; then they convinced the contractor (Tysons) for Phase 2 to lay the foundations, again as a gesture of goodwill. They persuaded the brick suppliers for Phase 2 to throw in the bricks; and Marks and Spencer to contribute the carpets.

Despite all this ingenuity, however, they still needed £450,000 of capital for the builder and some of the basic building materials. Tony, as manager of the old club at the time, recalls being approached by a major brewery, which presented him with a cheque for £250,000 towards the building costs. Attached to this 'generous' offer, of course, was a set of conditions and targets for beer sales that could have meant that, in time, the brewery would own the building. Tony

The Jubilee Hall and its manager, Tony McGann, with Rita Potter

Happy times in the new Village Hall

refused their offer, preferring to take the risk that the new business would be a financial success. On this basis, he and Margaret approached the bank that was underwriting the costs for part of the Phase 2 development. They agreed to lend the Eldonians £300,000.

The Board then asked all the residents of Phase 2 to agree to a £2 increase in their weekly rent, which would go towards the cost of the new building. If agreed, and when capitalized, this would provide the remaining £150,000. Everyone agreed, although in the event the final tender for the construction of the new houses came in under budget which meant that even with the £2 increase, the rent level would be as originally quoted to the new tenants.

The new club was opened in 1993 and it too is a highly successful community business – so much so that the bank loan has since been repaid. It was this type of 'flying by the seat of your pants' approach to most things during their early years that made the Eldonians so much fun to work with.

Sports facilities

This was the last of the main new facilities that the Development Trust created during Margaret's time with the Eldonians, and the funding stream was more straightforward – a bid to the Sports Lottery. In fact, this was the first *community* Sports Lottery funded project in the country. The result, in 1998, was a sports hall, a bowling green and an artificial sports pitch, and training for local people in sports development and management so that they could be employed to manage the centre.

Extra care sheltered scheme for the elderly

Leaping to the present, the source of funding for the Eldonians' latest development indicates their financial strength today. In 2007 the CBHA opened its latest care home for the elderly, costing £3.7m, which offers 24-hour care in 36 units. They acquired a grant from the Housing Corporation of £2.7m, took out a loan of £620,000 and contributed £380,000 from their own Reserve Fund. When the Prime Minister, Gordon Brown, opened it in June 2007, he said that the Eldonian Village was a 'model for the rest of the country'. In fact, he remarked to Tony McGann that he could not believe that the village was eighteen years old.

Prime Minister Gordon Brown and Tony share a joke at the opening of Robert Lynch House

This is where our story of the Eldonian journey ends, taking us full circle to Chapter 1, which sets out where they are now and their aspirations for the future. The final chapter looks at the lessons the Eldonian experience offers to other groups that want to create their own self-regenerating community; and concludes with reflections by those who worked alongside them and became their friends.

14 Lessons and Reflections

A HISTORICAL NARRATIVE has little value unless the people who come after are able to learn from it. And this story is no exception. What are the lessons from this extraordinary saga of transformation, and what has been the impact on the people who worked alongside the Eldonians?

Some lessons

In order to succeed, community-based organizations interested in developing more local control over their own neighbourhood, should:

Develop a vision

It is vital to have a clear vision of the ultimate goal. This vision must be developed and owned by all those who live in the area, or at least a large majority. The best visions are simple and can be limited to less than 25 words. It is not something that can be drawn up by consultants working for the landlord.

Create projects

From the vision comes programmes and from them come projects. Funding bodies still prefer to allocate resources to an ongoing programme of improvement, as Max Steinberg explained, as this leads to a critical mass that in time makes the neighbourhood more sustainable. So, the organization must have an annual flow of projects that it takes to decision makers for funding. The group's professionals will help put these projects together in a format for presentation.

Have a clear focus

Community organizations need to be focused, single-minded and determined to keep going, particularly when they have suffered setbacks. To remain focused, it is necessary to have strong leadership from the community. While there may not be too many Tony McGanns around, this type of single-mindedness is essential.

Be active in local politics

Do not be afraid of politics. Community organizations that are determined not to become 'victims' of decisions made within a local political machine need to be active within this structure – in England this is through their own ward party. I have too often heard members of groups saying they were leaving 'because this is getting political'. If you are trying to attract limited resources to your neighbourhood, then it *is* political. Being active in local politics also offers the opportunity to develop important networks at both the local and national level.

Getting involved in their local ward party was one of the key changes that the Eldonians brought about by and for themselves; to ensure that they were directly represented in the Town Hall. Key members of the community may belong to different political parties; this does not have to be a problem. What is important is that the community is represented in the local structures. Until the Eldonians took an active role, their local ward party did not fully represent them.

Enlist professional help

The Eldonians, for all their commitment, needed the advice and help of professionals. They recruited people on *their* terms, and they chose people who were able, committed to their cause, and keen to increase the capacity of their 'clients'. Communities can commission professionals, even if they are funded by someone else.

Acquire local assets

Power and influence come from owning and managing assets. Community organizations that wish to have influence must eventually acquire local assets, particularly housing. The Eldonian organization owns all its houses, the land and the facilities. Housing stock transfer is a common development in the UK today, and if housing bodies truly wish to empower local neighbourhoods, they need to transfer the ownership of the houses to organizations operated by local people. This will take time, but it is feasible, as the Eldonians have shown.

Initiate partnerships

It is important to be part of networks that lead to investment in the neighbourhood. It is equally important not to waste time sitting in on other people's partnerships that bring no local benefits.

Take stock

All successful organizations from time to time will review their performance against the targets they have set for themselves. Similarly, a successful neighbourhood organization will take stock of where it is going and how well it is doing. There are good professionals who can help with this. The review may lead to decisions to abandon some projects and refocus on new, more achievable ones. This is not defeat; it is good business.

Publicize your successes

It is part of the life-blood of a community to ensure that everyone knows about its successes. It helps to attract new members and to remind funders about what a good job the community is doing with their money. As important is to celebrate on a regular basis. We heard Rita Potter explain about the close link between the endless meetings and ending up at 2 o'clock in the morning dancing in their 'overalls'. The Eldonians never miss an opportunity to celebrate their successes.

Take every opportunity to learn

Finally, every one of us needs to learn from our own and other people's experiences. Take note of the critical factors in successes and failures; keep in touch with like-minded organizations, visit them and develop alliances with them.

Reflections

Finally, some reflections from the professionals who played and still play a key role in the Eldonian story. What do they think of the Eldonians' achievements, and what personal impact have the Eldonians had on their lives?

First, **Jim Dunne** who, as their priest, was their spiritual leader. The Eldonians hold Jim in high regard to this day, but he is convinced that they would have achieved all they did with or without the Church:

> I think what might have happened is it would have taken perhaps longer. In a way we were the oil that made things run smoothly... But I've always felt that what really did the trick was something that was quite negative – there comes a time when, if you ride roughshod over people, they will get up and say 'that's enough, stop it'. That time had come, and the threat to pull down the tenements *would* have sparked off such a violent resistance that the city council would have had to back down. They should be given credit for that.

Old friends: left to right: Rita Potter, Jim Dunne, Alice White and Lillian Grimes

The experience of working closely with this group of people also had a deep effect on Jim. He said that his years with the Eldonians enriched his life:

> They bore out some of my deepest instincts and beliefs… If you want to enable people it's very easy to do it in one sense; and the easy bit is to realize that there will be a hundred opportunities every day. The hard bit is the boundaries – it's when you stop being the oil and you want to do the moving yourself. So that was the first thing – it enabled me to fulfil things that I believed in.

The name that professionals today would give to Jim's role is 'capacity building'. He gives us a personal insight into the tremendous gift that the community gives to the enabler; and the caution that enablers, however committed they are to a cause, must resist the temptation to take over.

Jim recalls another significant gift from the Eldonians. As a priest, he believed that his most important function was to provide the liturgy (the ritual of a church service, including the symbols, words and music) in a way that related to people's lives; and he still remembers with joy the day that Tony came to him and said 'I think it's about time we had a Mass to celebrate all this':

> And I thought 'That's it!' *I* didn't say it to him, *he* said it to *me*! And I thought that means that he sees this as a rightful expression of what's been going on. And I thought that's what liturgy is about; a reflection of what's really happening; and if the liturgy is not picking up what's *really* happening to people, then it's just a charade.

Bill Halsall, the Eldonians' architect, looks back now and recognizes that 'the Eldonians were on a journey, and I was on a journey. They intersected at a point and that, in a way, was very productive for both parties – I hope!' He is confident that their achievements have permanence – the organization is secure for the future and will continue to develop new ideas and provide new facilities. He believes that the structure of the various parts of the organization and the quality of the staff will stand them in good stead for the future. Reflecting on what can be learned from the experience, he is curious as to why their structure and developments have not been replicated anywhere else in the UK. The Eldonians are a powerful example of how a rundown area can be rebuilt around a large social housing programme, which then draws in developers to provide housing for sale. He is convinced their structure of 'social ownership' – where the public housing is owned by the community and operates alongside private housing – has much to offer housing organizations and policy makers today, including the government's current long-term programme to restore the local housing market in some of the UK's poorest areas – the Housing Market Renewal Programme.

Max Steinberg could be described as the Eldonians' 'banker', playing a key role in helping to secure the funds for their housing schemes. Over the years he has developed a deep understanding of them and of the significance of their achievements:

> Success for me, looking back from 2007, is that Phase 1 still looks as if it was built last year. It looks and feels like a new development. All the schemes have retained that freshness, that sense of being part of something new; due to the way they handle the site and their attention to detail. There is no graffiti! You compare that with some other areas undergoing regeneration, good as they are, and look at the incidence of neglect. The Eldonians are very quick to deal with those things. It's a place you want to be.

Max recalls that it was witnessing the Eldonians' attention to detail and their wider agenda that led him to coin the phrase 'Housing Plus', a term that is now widely used among housing organizations:

> For me the village is an example of how housing-led regeneration can act as a *catalyst* to bring in the other socio-economic programmes that will take forward that regeneration – leisure and education; the private money that went into the nursery was attracted in because of the matched public money; housing for outright ownership where it didn't need shared-ownership support; the retail that came in.

He cites the local school, which has seen a significant improvement in performance at Key Stage 1 and Key Stage 2,[1] largely on the back of the housing investment; and the significant drop in the recorded crime figures from 1980 through to 2000:

> They have created the critical mass of a village in a city, which in my view is sustainable in the long term, remains attractive and compelling;

1 The two key stages in the National Curriculum for 5–11-year-old schoolchildren in Britain.

> and the facilities that support everyday life – social housing, educational facilities, opportunities for sport and leisure and business – now all co-exist side-by-side with each other. And *that's* what we get wrong from time to time. Single-faceted regeneration is almost inevitably bound to fail. The Eldonian Village provides a model for sustainable communities.

In Max's view, one can trace a clear progression from their work in the 1980s, through the government's Sustainable Communities Plan of the 1990s, to today – and the lessons of the Eldonians are as relevant today as they were in 1981. He pays particular tribute to Tony McGann:

> The personality, drive, commitment, curmudgeonly nature from time to time, and good humour of somebody who's now my friend, Tony McGann, has been immeasurably important. The fact that he can have Ministers, Secretaries of State, the two most senior Church leaders and a poor country-boy official from Liverpool, like me, bemused and bewitched, is testimony to his ability to do what he's done. So, there are lessons we *have* learnt, there are lessons that inform policy, and there are still lessons to learn from it if we're willing to do so.

Finally, Max sums up the personal impact of his years with the Eldonians:

> I never ever go there without coming away with a very personal quiet feeling of pride that I played a little part in achieving all this. Before my dad passed away they very kindly named a Court in my name. I was very touched by this unnecessary but thoughtful compliment. I'm grateful that people very close to me know that my input to the development was valued by a community with whom I developed a close and personal relationship.

Margaret Jackson, the first manager of the Eldonian Development Trust, went on to run a New Deal for Communities Programme, Single Regeneration Budget Programmes, and a Housing Market Renewal Programme, so like Max, her knowledge and experience of regeneration programmes is significant. She comments:

> These are the programmes that I've seen come and go, some of which have been more successful than others. More than anything I came to

> realize the importance of a shared vision. People must have a vision and a determination to achieve it, and the Eldonians are the perfect example of that.

Margaret is clear that there is no complete comparison to the Eldonian Village in the UK. As the former head of one of the government's Housing Market Renewal Pathfinders, she has had first-hand experience of trying to reverse a depressed local housing market, and make a place where people want to come and live. In her view, two of the best examples are the Castle Vale Housing Action Trust in Birmingham and the Eldonian Village:

> It's way up there just because it brings the jigsaw together in terms of housing, facilities, community involvement, and trying to get people involved in the training and management of housing services and health and leisure facilities. And because they were brought together in the building of the village, and now in its management, it's got a cohesion and a sustainability that others just don't have. People today talk about the jigsaw coming together to create a sustainable community. When that structure is constructed by a number of different agencies, it often doesn't quite ever click into place. The Eldonians created their own jigsaw and, therefore, it did click into place. There are so many lessons for elsewhere.

She believes that the Eldonians can teach other communities some lessons that are not to be found in the neat toolkits about neighbourhood regeneration:

> Just having that vision, holding on to it and still holding on to it; their determination; their ability to grow and learn and be politically savvy; have a can-do attitude; don't moan – they never moaned – and have a good laugh... They don't have a chip on their shoulders.

I, too, have always been impressed by the fact that despite the 'bum deal' they got in terms of local jobs, poor housing and the general state of their neighbourhood, they never blamed anyone else for this. But when the opportunity presented itself to take matters into their own hands, they seized it and have never let go.

Assessing the impact of Tony McGann, Margaret says:

> He was absolutely the head of steam; a terrier who was not going to let go. Tony has the rare ability to go into a meeting, have a real argument with somebody, stand his ground, but be able to end the meeting with a laugh, a joke and a shake of the hand. There are few people who can do that. He has a huge number of skills underpinned by this determination, and so he provides the leadership of his community. These skills in a local leader are very fundamental.

Like the rest of us who have worked with Tony over the years, Margaret remembers her ten years there with great fondness. We all got caught up in the excitement of it all and it was always good fun. However, as she reminds us:

> You couldn't slack! Because if you did, you'd have somebody called McGann on the phone, giving you a flea in the ear! – so there was a carrot and a stick working with the Eldonians, from a professional point of view!

Finally, she says that Tony has an instinct for presenting his messages to the outside world that makes the *community* feel good about itself – they are forever reading about themselves in the Press!

George Evans, of course, still works for the Eldonians as the Director of Housing of the CBHA. He has been involved with the Eldonians since the late 1970s. His first contact with them was while he was working for the city council; and then he worked alongside them during his years at Merseyside Improved Houses. Like the rest of us who have worked for or with them, they soon won his heart. He recalls the time he decided to tell his boss, Barry Natton at MIH, that he was going to work full-time for the Eldonians. Natton responded: 'To be honest, George, your heart's always been over there. We tried to get you to think about other things, but you were always drifting back over there!'

As he is still working there, George regards the whole of the Eldonian Village and its plans for the future as a 'work in progress'. His assessment of their achievements is measured:

> The list of achievements we have is as long as your arm, but the only two that made any difference to me are that, one, we managed to keep the community together; and two, we've given them a better quality of life than they had before. We've got to keep aiming to improve the quality

Celebrating 25 years of Eldonian success. Left to right: Jim Dunne, Jack McBane, Bill Halsall and Tony McGann.

> of life. The rest, such as the number of people we've managed to get into employment, the businesses we've set up, the number of awards we've achieved, mean nothing. *I* want to see this area do better on employment, do better on health, do better on education.

No sign of complacency there!

Lord Jenkin, the Secretary of State for the Environment between 1983 and 1985, says:

> I think their achievements have been staggering, and the fact that they've kept going, and that they have the kind of reputation that they have, is a huge tribute to Tony McGann, in particular, but also to all those who've been working with him. One wishes it could be replicated more frequently elsewhere. I think it's absolutely marvellous that somebody's going to write a book about it!

In the spirit of 'the first shall be last', I now offer my own thoughts as the first person to have worked with the Eldonians. I felt an instant rapport with them, particularly with Tony McGann, and I have often wondered since about the chemistry between us, and why our collaboration worked so well. When I met them I had been in England for nine years, and in that time I had grown angry at the level of poverty I saw. I had worked with communities in poor places, trying to instil in them a belief that they deserved better, and a confidence to take action. The Eldonians, in contrast, were a joy to meet because they already believed in themselves; they had already started to take action; and they knew what kind of help they needed. They reminded me of the people from the village of Quyon in Quebec, Canada, where I grew up; and our bond was both instant and deep. And Tony and I were kindred spirits. We both said what we thought and enjoyed good humour and a 'quick half'; and we shared a deep streak of determination.

When I first met them, I saw a group of people who felt that they had been bullied too often, and had for too long been on the wrong end of other people's decisions. I was also hit by the contrast between the appalling squalor of the 'public realm' and their powerful sense of belonging. As Margaret Jackson reminds us, they never moaned about their state, or had a chip on their shoulders.

My main contribution was to give them a vision of what the entire neighbourhood could become, and convince Tony that we should regard the long-term development of the whole area as our objective, with a series of projects along the way. To his great credit, he agreed, although I was not convinced that he felt confident about this at the outset.

We have been close friends since 1982, with the occasional argument along the way. Despite a career of thirty-five years in urban regeneration, and although I worked directly with the Eldonians for only three years, I feel this was the most profound work I did. They gave me an opportunity to express myself by putting into practice some long-held ideas about neighbourhood and belonging. Like Max, every time I visit them and remind myself of what they have achieved, I always leave inspired, full of hope, and privileged to have been a part of their journey.

Their distance travelled between 1976, when they stood up to the local Church hierarchy, to today is greater and more significant than any community in the UK that I am aware of. The Eldonian Village is the best example of the complete transformation of a slum neighbourhood in the UK. All the more so because the local people are still in control and they are not yet finished.

I believe that the village presents today's housing companies, registered social landlords, arm's length management organizations and local authorities with a model of how they could transfer control of neighbourhoods and their assets to the people who live in them. Communities can be empowered, not by an endless stream of development workers, but by corporate ownership of the assets of their houses and local facilities. One of the key reasons for the influence of the Eldonians today is their asset base. They are active in partnerships as investment partners, not simply as some local community group.

As George explains, while there is more to be done, the most fundamental elements of a 'sustainable community' are in place, and they brought these about by constantly striving to improve the quality of life of the people who live in the village and around it. It is not that the Eldonian Village meets the criteria for a sustainable community, it is that the Academy for Sustainable Communities developed criteria that match the country's best example!

The last word on this story of the Eldonians must go to Tony McGann, their leader and inspiration since 1976. About their future, he has this to say:

We haven't even taken our coats off here!

Appendix 1: The Cast

A NUMBER OF RESIDENTS, and the professionals who have worked closely with them, appear in this book, usually accompanied by a brief biography. The list below may be useful in minimizing confusion as the story unfolds. They are not listed in order of appearance.

Residents of the Eldonian Village

Tony McGann was born and grew up in the Vauxhall area and has lived there all his life. He has been the leader of the Eldonians for the last thirty years. He is also the manager of their social club.

Joan McGann is Tony's wife. She led the residents' design committee for Phase 1 of the village. She has also lived all her life in the Vauxhall area.

Rita Potter, Lilian Grimes and **Eileen O'Brien** all grew up in the area. They discuss both life in the old tenements, and the early days of the formation of the Eldonians.

Margaret Dragonette was born and grew up in the tenements on Eldon Street. Her father, Michael, played a key role in the early days. Margaret is now the secretary of the Eldonian CBHA.

Frank Brady, Lynn Burke, Marie Ryan and **Linda Coburn** have lived in the village since it opened in 1989 and they discuss what it is like living there today.

Residents from the former housing co-op at Portland Gardens

John Livingston and **Billy Little** lived in Portland Gardens and played leading roles in the development of the Portland Gardens housing co-operative. Billy has since died, and John lives in one of the houses from the former co-op.

Billy Little junior is Billy Little's son, who has memories of his parents' excitement and enthusiasm as they committed to the Portland Gardens co-op. He also now lives in Portland Gardens.

Peggy Hackett has also lived in the area all her life. She too lives in a house in Portland Gardens.

The professionals

Jim Dunne grew up in a tenement in the Vauxhall area. He was the Catholic priest for Our Lady's church on Eldon Street. He has since left the priesthood and lives with his wife Ruth in the north-east of England.

George Evans was born and grew up in Liverpool. He worked initially in the Housing Department of Liverpool City Council, where he first met the Eldonians. He joined them full-time in 1993 and is today their Director of Housing.

Bill Halsall was also born and raised in Liverpool. He is an architect who has worked with the Eldonians since 1982, and has designed all the main buildings in the village. He has his own practice, based in Liverpool, where he lives.

Margaret Jackson was employed by the Liverpool Housing Trust as a landscape architect, and worked for the Eldonian Development Trust (Eldonian Group) from the mid-1980s for ten years. She led on the development of many of the 'non-housing' facilities in the village. She works today as a management consultant.

Jack McBane, the author, was the first professional to work alongside the Eldonians, in 1982. He is today semi-retired, works part-time as a management consultant, and lives with his wife, Jane, in Sheffield, South Yorkshire

Lawrence Santangeli has historical connections to this area of Liverpool. When his family first came to England from Italy in the 1800s, they settled in Vauxhall; and he was born and brought up in nearby Bootle. He began working in regeneration in 1991, and joined the Eldonians in 2000 as their Property and Business Development Manager. He is today the Chief Executive of the Eldonian Group.

Max Steinberg, another Liverpool boy, worked for the Housing Corporation in the city from 1978 to 2003. Max played a key role in the funding of the village, and has been a strong supporter of the Eldonians for over twenty years.

Appendix 2: Tributes

While this book was in production, Tony McGann wrote to a number of people asking if they would like to contribute their reflections on the Eldonians. In the main, these were people who do not appear directly in this story, but who the Eldonians either associated with and worked with in the past, or work with today. The response was tremendous, with many thoughtful tributes. This appendix contains excerpts from these tributes, with some commentary on their context.

Councillor Joe Anderson, Leader of the Labour Group, Liverpool City Council

Councillor Joe Anderson has known the Eldonians since their early days and has followed their progress with interest. Today he is the Leader of the Labour Group on Liverpool City Council. This used to be a fractured and, at times, bitter relationship, as we saw in the story, but this is now in the past, and is a sign of how the Eldonians continue to grow and make new alliances. He writes:

> As a councillor, and Leader of the Labour Party here in Liverpool, I passionately believe in community development through people taking control and shaping their own and their community's future. The Eldonian project is an inspiration to me and to many others as an example that shows very clearly how this works. The mixture of affordable social housing to rent and houses for sale is a model that

truly works. There are many strands required to make communities feel safe and secure and the people in them feel they belong. The Eldonian village offers this and much much more.

I want to make sure that the Eldonian project continues and grows from strength to strength and is replicated in other areas across the city. The ethos and community spirit is recognized throughout the world and they rightly received the World Habitat Award for their hard work and dedication to real inclusion and community development.

The Eldonian concept was the first to truly understand and practise social inclusion, and their leaders instantly recognized that regeneration meant not just the physical environment, but that of the community and its people. That's why the village with its sports centre, its nursery, the village hall and the sheltered accommodation, provide services for the community by the community, and that's why it will always be successful because of community involvement.

The Eldonian organization truly is a remarkable achievement and its future is secure; it has not and will not rest on its laurels; it moves on recognizing the importance of meeting the new demands and needs of its community. It has ambitious plans for now and the future that will help sustain, develop and continue the spirit that created this marvellous concept. Their champion Tony McGann and all those involved should be proud of the achievements so far, but there is so much more to come. The legacy of the Eldonians will not be just the transformation of industrial wasteland and abandoned docks. The legacy will be a thriving organization with vision and the same passion, who are determined to continue the spirit and hard work of those who pioneered such a great institution.

Diane Diacon, Director of the UK-based Building and Social Housing Foundation

The Foundation coordinates the annual World Habitat Award on behalf of the United Nations. Their Director writes:

The Building and Social Housing Foundation is more than happy to endorse the work of the Eldonians and we wish you every success with the forthcoming publication.

Already well known in the UK, the Eldonians' work was internationally recognized when it received the World Habitat Award in 2004.

This long-standing and internationally renowned award recognizes innovative and sustainable housing practice around the world, and the submission presented by the Eldonians was a worthy winner.

The judges of the Award recognized that not only had a small group of local people managed to keep their community together in the face of threatened demolition and dispersal, they had also provided good-quality homes in an attractive environment. Not content with having improved their own living conditions, they went on to address wider issues faced by the community in their local area, providing over 100 permanent jobs in business enterprises, as well as recreation, child-care and older persons' care opportunities.

The determination and commitment of the Eldonians are an example to all communities around the world who wish to improve their living conditions and have a greater say in their future.

With every best wish to you and your colleagues for the Eldonians' continuing work and success.

Lady Grace Sheppard

Lady Grace Sheppard was the wife of Bishop David Sheppard, who was a strong supporter and friend of the Eldonians from the outset. Lady Sheppard often accompanied her husband on his visits to the Eldonians. She writes:

Just occasionally in life something happens which rings a clear bell as if to say, 'Yes. This rings true.' The Eldonians had found a secret of creating a confident community that made sense and which has lasted. Vision was put into practice. Here was faith and action perfectly combined. We were privileged to witness its beginnings.

It is many years since I had the privilege of visiting the Eldonian Village on the old Tate & Lyle site by the docks. The first time I was invited was alongside David, my husband, Bishop of Liverpool at the time, and his colleague and friend Archbishop Derek Worlock and his chaplain, Mgr John Furnival. We were shown round every nook and cranny and encouraged to ask questions of anyone.

The memory of that visit has remained strong and vivid in every respect. There was a welcome, enthusiasm and pride. Trust, imagination, cooperation and sheer hard work were also part of the magic mix. Tony McGann and his team welcomed us so warmly. Then came the infectious enthusiasm from the other residents, and the pride. They were proud of their new homes and community. There was a place for everyone. No-one was excluded. Local people had agreed to see their old homes... razed to the ground, in trust. They knew that not only were they invited to help in the design of their new homes and community, but also that they were assured that they could have the same neighbours. Their talents were harnessed so that everyone had a part to play. The houses were not in rows, but in clusters. What inspiration and vision this represented! A whole community was lifted from one area to another with mutual agreement and collaboration.

I remember being struck with the sensitivity and common sense that this approach represented. Foundations were laid which were not only bricks and mortar but good communication and genuine collaboration. The chosen firm of architects spent many hours listening to the community before going to the drawing board; and throughout the project they agreed to work with the residents and with other disciplines. It meant a great deal of hard work and patience from everyone. A mammoth job of coordination and perseverance was done by Tony McGann. He also had to give account to the press, as he became the spokesperson. Later this was extended as people became interested worldwide. He is still there over twenty years later.

Then came the pride – the proper pride in the imaginative achievement. This was Liverpool at its best. There had been mutual respect in the planning and the execution. That they thought of involving the churches was far-sighted, courageous and touching in an area where there had been bitter feuding in the past between Catholic and Protestant. They were challenging days politically in Liverpool at that time, and the bishops provided encouragement and support. They in turn were thrilled and inspired with what they saw and heard. The sugar from Tate & Lyle's had gone, but something far sweeter had arisen. To cap it all the Eldonians had the grace to say thank you to the two bishops on a banner held high over the street, which said 'Thank you – we did it Better Together', which became the title of a book that the two wrote later, suitably credited. There is no better motto for the rest of us. God bless the Eldonians!

Peter Kilfoyle, MP

Peter Kilfoyle, MP, was born in Liverpool and represents the Walton constituency in the city. He has been a friend of Tony McGann's for many years and has admired the work of the Eldonians over that time. He writes:

> From the relatively small beginnings of a threat to their homes… sprang a unique phenomenon in the rich varied history of Liverpool. The community in and around Eldon Street… banded together to save their homes and to keep their community together in the area. This led directly to the Eldonians – a powerful driver of local regeneration. Not just new houses, but jobs, training, and social facilities. It is a model which has earned plaudits and prizes nationally and internationally.
>
> From a wider perspective, there are many lessons to be drawn from the Eldonian experience about what the word 'community' actually means, and how 'community' might organize itself. If nothing else, the Eldonians are living proof that the community that works together can stay together for the mutual benefit.

Lord Professor David Alton

During the 1970s, David Alton was a Liberal member of Liverpool City Council. He sat on its Housing Committee and in 1978 became its Chairman. Among the policies that he promoted at that time was support for housing cooperatives, self-build developments and low-cost homes for sale. In 1978 he also initiated the programme of renewal and replacement of many of the city's tenements, including Vauxhall. After his election to Parliament in 1979 he regularly cited the example of the Eldonians as the model that others should follow. He writes:

> It wasn't just that I believed in housing cooperatives. I also believed in the grit and the spirit which was represented by Tony McGann and the Eldonian community.
>
> It was a difficult time in Liverpool's history and the menacing intimidation which became the hallmarks of the Militant Tendency were directed with all their force at the non-compliant Eldonians. Here was a community who refused to be bullied into submission; who defied the diktat to be sent to the four corners of Liverpool, and who were determined to keep their community together. They fought the council with courage, shrewd ingenuity and resilience.
>
> Their determination gathered an array of supporters, from illustrious members of the Royal family, to the city's bishop and Archbishop, and just as importantly, their refusal to 'give in' gave hope to the ordinary men and women in the street.

Perhaps the protracted and bruising nature of that fight is the key to understanding why the Eldonian development has been so successful. Cooperatives give people a real stake in the ownership and management of their homes but, in this case, every brick had been fought over. When in life things come too easily people tend to take them for granted. That could never be said of the Eldonians.

Right Honourable Paddy Ashdown

Paddy Ashdown was formerly the Leader of the Liberal Democrat Party. Towards the end of his time in this position, he undertook a tour of Britain to visit a wide range of places and hear from the people who lived there. One of his stops was the Eldonian Village. He writes:

> I am delighted that you are having a book written about the Eldonians. It is important that all your achievements are laid out — if only to serve as an inspiration to others.
>
> One of the great trends of our age is self help. The days of Big Governments doing things FOR people are over. Just look at things like Wikipedia and You-Tube and you see that what people want is not to be told what to do, but to have the tools to be able to do things for themselves. The Eldonians were one of the very early pioneers in this field. What they achieved was not just helping individuals but also acting as an inspiration to others and a catalyst for others to follow their lead. I wish you all the very best for the future.

Tom Penn, Head of Family Health Services Support, NHS Central Operations, Liverpool

Tom Penn has known the Eldonians for over twenty years. He writes:

> I first became aware of their existence and the tremendous work carried out by them through contact with the Chair of the Eldonians, Tony McGann, in his role as a Non-Executive Director of the Family Health Services Authority and subsequently its successor body Liverpool Health Authority. Tony to this day remains actively involved in health matters continuing as Chair of the Pharmacy Contracts Committee... What did impress me some twenty years ago, and continues to impress me to this day, is the vision and commitment this community has to

make things happen and bring about the necessary changes which will affect not just themselves but their children and, I have no doubt, their children's children...

All these achievements have been made against the odds by a community which at the outset suffered from some of the worst housing, poverty, unemployment and ill health not just across Liverpool but across the whole country. Against this background their achievements are even more remarkable.

What has never ceased to amaze me is the drive and enthusiasm that this community has to make their vision a reality; but perhaps more important is that they have had the strength of purpose and organization not only to sustain their vision but to build upon it... Walk around the streets of the village, go into the village hall and the sports centre, and although you cannot see it you can certainly feel it, and that is the real sense of community and community spirit that is in abundance here.

I am very aware that the Eldonian Association have for many years recognized the crucial link between good housing, employment, the social and physical environment, and health. I know that as part of its continued vision the Eldonians are looking with other agencies and authorities as to how they can improve both the access to, and the range of, health services both locally within their own community and also to the surrounding area. I have no doubt that whatever the obstacles and difficulties before them they will undoubtedly achieve their goal. The Eldonian Community Association is the finest example of what can be achieved when a whole community comes together with a common goal and purpose. Long may they continue.

Louise Ellman, MP

Louise Ellman is the MP for Liverpool Riverside, which includes the Eldonian Village. Since her election as an MP, she has been a close friend and supporter of the Eldonians. She writes:

I am delighted to learn that the Eldonians' story is being recorded. The Eldonians have made a magnificent contribution to urban renewal and inner city regeneration. This has been achieved on the basis of commitment to community, cooperation and enterprise. Achievements include providing housing, facilities for the young and the old, and pioneering safety projects. Dereliction has been replaced by innovative regeneration.

The Eldonians' achievements have transformed the lives of thousands of people providing a model for regeneration. That is why you have received national and international recognition.

Your own leadership is inspiring and I feel privileged to have the Eldonians in my constituency.

Phil Gandy, Group Chief Executive, Vicinity Housing Group

As we heard from Margaret Jackson, the Eldonians have enjoyed a productive working relationship with Liverpool Housing Trust. Today LHT is part of a wider housing organization, Vicinity. Its Chief Executive, Phil Gandy, writes:

> Liverpool Housing Trust (LHT) has strong links with the Eldonians going back many years. During that time, as both organizations have developed and grown, we have seen the Eldonians established as a model of excellence in both housing and community regeneration, a model that has deservedly drawn plaudits and awards locally, nationally and internationally.
>
> We are proud that, as LHT and more recently the Vicinity Group, acting as a friend and partner we have been able to play a small part in supporting and helping you achieve your aspirations and ambitions on behalf of your community. We look forward to many more years of working in partnership with the Eldonians, cooperating to deal with the fresh challenges that may lie ahead, and using the strengths of both our organizations to take advantage of the many opportunities that I am confident will also arise for us in the future.

Deborah Shackleton, Chief Executive, Riverside Housing

Merseyside Improved Houses played a key role in the development of the Eldonians. It was my employer and it stood by the Eldonians during their early years. It is now a larger organization called Riverside Housing. Its current Chief Executive, Deborah Shackleton, writes:

> We are proud to have been associated with the Eldonians for over twenty years as agents, supporters and friends. You are true Liverpool

pioneers, from the earliest days when the founders had to overcome barrier after barrier through sheer force of will and personality, to later years when you have been able to spread your wings and deliver a wide range of neighbourhood services. Terms such as community architecture, secure by design, neighbourhood management and housing plus, didn't exist 'back then', and it is the innovative work of local people in your community which has paved the way for so much of what is now established practice.

As we are well aware, you don't take 'no' for an answer! But it is this independence and determination which marks you out, and which has been the foundation of your amazing success. We wish you all the best for the future, knowing that you will continue to serve the people of Vauxhall with passion and commitment.

Jane Kennedy, MP

Jane first learned of the Eldonians through members of her trade union, the National Union of Public Employees, in 1982, when she was a newly elected Branch Secretary. As some of her members lived in the Portland Gardens Housing Co-op, she learned about how their new scheme had been taken from them by the city council. She writes:

> To their shock and dismay, after being closely involved in the design and build of their new homes – following generations living in tenement blocks – these members of my union were horrified when the newly elected Labour council, dominated by the Militant Tendency, announced that the housing cooperative was to be 'municipalized'. They would lose the first opportunity they had ever had to own their homes and influence the way in which they were managed...
>
> The Eldonians are now and were then an honest expression of a genuine grass-roots cooperative response to the problem of chronic shortages of new, good quality housing in the city...
>
> I wish that Eldon Street had been in my constituency. The courage and determination that characterizes the Eldonians is founded upon a strong sense of the worth of their own community. If fostered and encouraged by the local authority it could have enabled lasting improvements in neighbourhoods across the city....
>
> Thank goodness that successive governments, not least this Labour government, recognized the value of their achievements: new homes

> providing the bedrock of a more secure, respectful and peaceful environment, for our elders to enjoy and young families to settle into for the long term. Bravo to the Eldonians.

Chris Farrow, former Chief Executive of the Merseyside Development Corporation (MDC)

Chris Farrow was the Chief Executive of the MDC at the time when the Corporation provided strong support and assistance to the Eldonians in the development of Phase 2 of the village. He writes:

> As the former Chief Executive of Merseyside Development Corporation you should know that it was one of the outstanding privileges, even in my hectic career, to have been able to support the Eldonians' total transformation of their community.
>
> In 1975 the then government's Community Action Programme highlighted this part of Liverpool as one of the most deprived and under pressure urban communities in the UK. Today it is an oasis of regeneration and a demonstration project in not only how to do regeneration, but how local and cooperative community leadership can achieve it for themselves. The Merseyside Development Corporation played a critical part in the physical regeneration of the area – a considerable challenge when it is remembered that the land beneath the feet of the Eldonians had itself suffered the ravages of four or five industrial revolutions. This kind of physical transformation did require a huge investment by the Corporation of money and skill. However, the above ground development and its management is probably the most brilliant exposition of urban regeneration of a neighbourhood in the UK.
>
> Although we are all now relieved and happy to forget this, we should also recall that the Eldonians' achievement was secured by this community at a time when many others in Liverpool were investing their time in either trying to bring down the government or standing on the sidelines watching this futile attempt.
>
> This is probably the key Eldonian message: Focus on what you want to achieve for yourselves, by yourselves; identify those things that will make the biggest transformation in the community; then identify a modest and practical first step forward; then relentlessly keep taking bigger and bigger steps until you reach your destination.

Gideon Ben-Tovim, Chair of Liverpool NHS PCT

Gideon is Reader in the Department of Sociology, University of Liverpool, and author of various books, reports and articles in the fields of race relations, regeneration, local government and education. He is an elected member of Liverpool City Council for Princes Park ward, and until recently was Chair of Liverpool Community College.

> I first became aware of the work of Tony McGann and the Eldonians in the 1980s during the period of struggles between many different communities and the then Militant regime at the city council. I was pleased to have been able to help forge an alliance at the time between the 'north end' and the 'south end' of the city in the shared quest for social justice and respect for independent community organizations. Tony showed the courage, innovation and leadership that have marked his community work.
>
> I have over the years had the opportunity of working with Tony on various issues. The Liverpool Community College, of which I was then Chair, was very pleased at the support Tony gave when the new college centre was established in Vauxhall. Road. The Eldonians have been an excellent neighbour and partner since then.
>
> As Chair of Liverpool NHS Primary Care Trust I have learnt of Tony's great interest and commitment to the health improvement as well as the educational advancement of young people in particular. Here again Tony has proven to be a passionate advocate for the local community.
>
> It has always been a privilege for me to know Tony and to work with him. I congratulate him on his personal achievements and wish the Eldonians many more successes in the years ahead.

Professor Peter Roberts, OBE, Chair of the Academy for Sustainable Communities

As we have seen, Peter Roberts has, in his professional capacity, assessed the Eldonians' achievements against the Academy's eight criteria for a sustainable community. He writes:

> It gives me great pleasure to be able to comment on the many achievements of the Eldonians, and to congratulate you and your colleagues on your outstanding record of success.

In many ways the work of the Eldonians exemplifies what can be achieved by a determined community working to a clear vision. The creation of a sustainable community in Vauxhall represents a model that others can use, and demonstrates that the impossible can be delivered, although it may take a little longer than initially expected.

The Academy for Sustainable Communities is delighted that it is able to draw upon your experience. You have provided hope and inspiration for others. Long may you continue your good work.

Bibliography

Belchem, John, 'Celebrating Liverpool', in John Belchem (ed.), *Liverpool 800: Culture, Character and History* (Liverpool University Press, 2006)

Diacon, Diane, and Silvia Guimarães, *Presentation of the World Habitat Awards* (Building and Social Housing Foundation, 2004)

Fagan, Ged, *Liverpool In A City Living* (Countyvise Limited, 2004)

Leeming, Karen, 'Sustainable Urban Development: A Case Study of "The Eldonians" in Liverpool', in Tasleem Shakur (ed.), *Cities in Transition: Transforming the Global Built Environment* (Open House Press, 2005)

Liverpool Echo, 'A Royal Day When Charles Came To Town', 4 May 1989, 13

Meegan, Richard, and Alison Mitchell, 'It's Not Community Round Here, It's Neighbourhood', *Urban Studies*, 38.12 (2001), 2167–94

Murden, Jon, 'City of Change and Challenge: Liverpool since 1945', in John Belchem (ed.), *Liverpool 800: Culture, Character and History* (Liverpool University Press, 2006)

Parkinson, Michael, *Liverpool on the Brink* (Policy Journals, 1985)

Roberts, Peter, 'Social Innovation, Spatial Transformation and Sustainable Communities: Liverpool and the Eldonians', in P. Drewe, E. Hulsbergen and J. Klein (eds), *The Challenge of Social Innovation in Urban Revitalisation* (Techne Press, 2007)

Royden, Mike W., 'The 19th Century Poor Law in Liverpool and its Hinterland: Towards the Origins of the Workhouse Infirmary', lecture given at the Liverpool Medical History/Historic Society of Lancashire and Cheshire Conference 'The Poor Law and After: Workhouse Hospitals and Public Welfare', 10 April 1999

Scally, Robert, *The End of Hidden Ireland* (Oxford University Press, 1995)

Sheppard, David, and Derek Worlock, *Better Together. Christian Partnership in a Hurt City* (Hodder & Stoughton, 1988)

Tarn, John, *Five Per Cent Philanthropy: An Account of Housing in Urban Areas between 1840 and 1914* (Cambridge University Press, 1973)